Educating Young Children

Educating Young Children
A Structural Approach

Helen McAuley & Peter Jackson

David Fulton Publishers
London
Published in association with the Roehampton Institute

David Fulton Publishers Ltd
2 Barbon Close, London WC1N 3JX

First published in Great Britain by
David Fulton Publishers 1992

British Library Cataloguing in Publication Data

A catalogue record for this book is available from the British Library

ISBN 1-85346-195-4

Typeset by Spectrum Typesetting Ltd, London E2
Printed in Great Britain by BPCC Wheaton Ltd, Exeter

Contents

Acknowledgements

We are grateful to the thought and practice of colleagues, both present and past. Few of those to have influenced our thinking are mentioned by name so here we express our thanks generally. We are equally indebted to In-Service students for their valuable co-operation in studying the research projects considered for this book and relating their implications to classroom practice. Thanks are due also to two of this year's Visiting Scholars – Professor Gene Phillips of Indiana State University and Professor Hideo Koizumi of Yokahama University – who brought welcome perspectives to our thinking. Finally we must thank for her energy, enthusiasm and encouragement the head of the Early Childhood Studies Centre here at Froebel Roehampton, Shirley Maxwell.

Introduction

Educational research has been neglected by many teachers of young children who said they would pay attention when it investigated real children in real classrooms. Now that the research arena has shifted to classrooms teachers would, we think, be interested to read and reflect on the findings and review their practice. Accordingly we have clustered some studies of young children learning and evaluated them.

We take a *structural* approach to our evaluation, meaning that we always try to place children's learning in contexts, emphasising relationships and what helps to form them. The method has something to do with continental structuralism (see Gibson, 1984), but not a lot. That movement seems over-complex and too heavily theoretical for our purposes. Our aims are essentially plain and practical and it is fitting that our methods match them in simplicity.

We stress that our approach is a method of reflection not a conclusion about how children should be educated. We have little in common with those educators who want teachers to build tight firm structures into their classroom arrangements. We lack enthusiasm for High/Scope and other even more strongly directive educational philosophies.

Young children between 3 and 6 years should be less rather than more hemmed in by rules and organization: they should be offered greater scope for spontaneity and imagination in the development of their work. The restraint and responsibility belong to teachers not to children. The former should so develop their sensitivity, skills and overall curricular and developmental understanding that they can confidently allow space and time for children to explore and experiment, secure in their professional knowledge that they can help when it is appropriate to do so.

Our focus is the tutorial relationship between pupil and teacher. It is the single most educationally significant structure in which teachers and pupils find themselves at school. Responsibility lies with teachers, entitlement with pupils. Teachers have to take the developing thought of pupils seriously, to guard against the tendency to fence in their ideas. By being clearer and more confident about the wider picture teachers should seek to preserve the space and time for children's initial explorations. Nowhere is this exhibited more clearly than in the tutorial, planned or spontaneous.

The book is in three sections. The central section contains the main evaluations of the research studies and the first and third seek to establish our framework of values.

SECTION ONE: TOWARDS A STRUCTURALIST CRITIQUE

CHAPTER 1
Education Theory

There is a general mistrust of theory among professionals in early childhood education, particularly theory urging change for obscure reasons. We are as suspicious of this as anyone. But we are at least as wary of the 'anything, as long as it works' mentality, which puts the emphasis on outcomes and rulers. Suspecting that tapes reduce what they measure, we fear that the noble idea of *educating* young children – hardly widely held in the UK and unknown in many parts of the globe – would all too easily shrink to training in behaviour or intellect.

Since we are offering professionals a book about educating young children we have to find some middle way. Our solution is to welcome research, particularly classroom research, while being sceptical about recommendations; to learn from the traditions of practice, while doubting the theory and to try, wherever possible, to see things whole.

This is a book about how schools can be educating structures. We have, after all, subtitled it 'a structural approach'. But readers who expect to find the clear stamp of the Continental and American structuralists will be disappointed. Though we take their central concern with structures to heart we don't follow a systematic approach. The writer we find most accessible is Piaget. Although we are less keen on his cognitive contribution to education than some of our colleagues are, we find his book *Structuralism* very helpful. Its warnings against a bitty analytic approach to criticism make us determined to look at structures and relationships, rather than particular things. Needless to say, we don't always follow that advice.

We try to look upon the school as a whole organism with philosophy, policies and practices. Some other approaches to the topic of educating young children have informed but not quite satisfied us. Examining separate research projects about teachers,

1

children, the curriculum or even teaching and learning seems too piecemeal. We can see advantages in that approach – greater precision, finer distinctions and so on – but we feel the larger picture gets lost. While our stance may be different from some others we try to ensure that the method of work remains reasonably familiar and straightforward. That is why we prefer to call our approach structural rather than structuralist.

We want first to draw the reader's attention to what we perceive as an important shift in the theoretical context of education. In the UK there are at least two distinct versions of education theory. What we dub Version One is the whipping boy of politicians and pundits. In the Press it is roundly condemned and blamed for all sorts of ills. It consisted largely of theories imported from the human sciences, especially psychology and sociology. These came clothed in specialist language, which needed unravelling and explaining. Questions of obscurity and irrelevance continually recurred.

A typical topic embedded in Education Theory Version One was 'verbal deficit'. The theory held that large sections of society were disadvantaged both materially and cognitively. The argument went something like this: in order to think successfully, concepts are necessary. Many of the more sophisticated concepts are given form and substance in language. Thus there must be adequate language development. Children's language developed, according to the dominant psychological theory, by the shaping and moulding contexts of their immediate families. Where the linguistic structures were elementary children's development suffered not only linguistically but cognitively.

The thesis was supported by a sociological theory holding that the linguistic codes which children learned in the home significantly affected their ability to learn in school. The children of large sections of society didn't learn to use at home the kind of codes which schools used. Thus they were disadvantaged by the very system which could have helped them. The two theories – psychological and sociological – intertwined to provide a powerfully insidious explanation of those results of large-scale surveys which revealed major differences between the academic achievements of the poorer classes whether in the UK or the USA, and the rest of the population.

This was from Education Theory Version One. Impossible for students to refute, it was a kind of theory that was based on theory. It was probably vulnerable only to yet more theory. It yielded only 'how' type questions. How could teachers help children who were already behind in their language and tools of thought? Devise specialist programmes like the Peabody Language Development Kit? Build on compensatory schemes? Adopt different methods? The theory had its theoretical critics of course. Theory feeds on theory. But one had to be a theorist to be able to evaluate the debates. All too often, positions would simply be taken up on ideological grounds.

We choose this as an example of Version One partly because of two papers in the early learning field which revisited that old debate and provide an illustration of a remarkable change in the research agenda for education. The change occurred in the mid-seventies and led to what we are calling Education Theory Version Two. The two papers are by Barbara Tizard and Martin Hughes: Hughes in Desforges 1989, Tizard and Hughes in Walford 1990. Both papers referred to the authors' joint research project into language at home and school published in 1984 as *Young Children Learning*.

The papers drew attention to a span of time. Although their project was published as a book in 1984 it was carried out from 1976-8 and planned in 1975. Thus the span from inception to their joint paper is sixteen years. That it seems even longer owes much to the fact that their own research project belonged to a research era markedly different from what established the verbal deficit theory in the sixties and early seventies. It now takes an effort to think back and appreciate the highly theoretical character of the verbal deficit theory Tizard and Hughes addressed.

Something clearly happened in the mid-seventies. Governments and other funding bodies began to distribute grants for projects designed to find out what was going on in schools. The research climate underwent a transformation. Hitherto what passed for education theories were sets of prescriptions taken from human science theories, themselves often precariously erected on slender empirical plinths. In the mid-seventies, however, the research emphasis changed to description and prescriptions were less and less confidently advanced.

A battery of investigations was funded by, amongst other bodies, DES, SED, DHSS, SSRC, the Schools' Council, Leverhulme and the Gulbenkian. In 1975 DES published a list of topics for research and development in the field of pre-school education and care, later funding the study of play and learning by Hutt and his colleagues. From 1973-78 Athey undertook her Froebel Nursery Project. In 1975 both the Oxford Pre-school Research Project and the ORACLE longitudinal research began. The Open University Nursery School Project into teaching styles and child behaviour also started at this time and was supplemented by the NFER and OU studies of nursery teachers.

Among many other projects the HMI undertook large-scale systematic evaluations of schools and school systems. It was in this climate that Tizard and Hughes conducted their project and reported findings which complemented small studies such as Labov (1969), Wight and Norris (1970) and Sinclair and Coulthard (1975) and the large-scale Bristol University findings of Gordon Wells in the late seventies and eighties, all at some odds with received opinions about verbal deficit. In her monumental 1988 book and numerous articles Margaret Clark reviewed much of the pre-school research and evidence of the seventies and early eighties, coming to the conclusion that narrowing and formalizing the curriculum and increasing assessment could 'confirm teachers in their belief in the limited expectations of children' (Brown and Wake, 1988, p.150).

It was not until the eighties – and in many cases the late eighties – that many of the studies were published in book form. At present there is a flood of reports from both large and small scale projects covering an impressively wide educational range, School effectiveness studies, teaching skills research, time management projects, governing body investigations, assessment comparisons, classroom interaction analysis: these are only a few of the topics researchers have addressed. The list is long, giving more information than we have ever had before.

Now, and probably for the first time, teachers and education policy makers have their own research store. It is as empirical and relevant and practically based as the Government and pundits and teachers could possibly wish for, and it is the basis of in-service courses. This body of evidence needs, in our opinion, close attention. It calls out for analysis and judgment. We want to call the processes and products of sifting and evaluating the findings of educationally relevant projects Education Theory Version Two. Interpreting the significance of the findings should begin now.

A pleasing feature of the new wave of research studies has been the cautiousness of the authors when it comes to recommendations. They have for the most part been reluctant to draw principles from their work and to urge policies. An illustration is provided by the Tizard and Hughes study already mentioned. In their 1991 paper the authors considered the general academic reaction to their project and responded to a particular critique in the *Harvard Educational Review* by Brice-Heath. In answer to one of her criticisms they display the new modesty

> ... the study was not of the kind that leads to simple recommendations. It set out to challenge received notions about what children might be learning at home and at nursery school, and to create an 'agenda for concern'. The findings do not in themselves imply that any specific educational practices are desirable, they are rather an invitation to think in a new way about these practices. If an opportunity had arisen for us to take part in such a rethinking with teachers, we would have taken it, but we would expect any innovations in practice that resulted to come from teachers. (Walford, 1991, p.36).

The invitation to reflect on the new research is what we take up. For us, that is the purpose of advanced inservice courses at this time. Students and tutors analyse, compare, try out, and discuss the implications of the studies, using their own professional understanding and experience. How should such evaluation be undertaken? Given that our aim is a positive one – to recommend principles for the practice of educating young children – we want to avoid the approaches to which we referred at the beginning of the chapter. Specifically we want to guard against the temptation to select for analysis simply what are considered to be the most important research projects in the field. We have consciously utilised a constructive reading of groups of projects trying, whenever possible, to focus on structures and their effects rather than individuals and their efforts. Our aim has been to compare and contrast research studies for their methods as well as for their findings.

We think of each individual research project as having two references. First there is the *vertical* reference to a state of affairs which the researchers seek to describe as accurately as possible, using a number of techniques. For example, a research project concerned to capture what is going on in conversations between mothers and young girls refers to a specific research location and has a particular research design. It may include such variables as the selection of the families, the recording methods, the presentation of the evidence, and so on. The claims advanced for the success of the project will be relevant to the valuation, as well as any expectations, declared or not, on the part of the researchers.

There ought perhaps to be a sort of Government Health Warning here: there is a tinge of structuralism about our belief that no vertical reference can yield the simple correspondence with the facts that crude empiricists expect. Unlike torches, research studies do not reveal what was hidden: in an important sense, they *make* their findings and any implications are, as a result, necessarily ambiguous. This is not radical scepticism, simply a statement that trustworthiness has to be judged in the light of many factors, something which is part of the academic outlook of good empiricist analysts. Unfortunately, all too frequently in this country, research projects get rather poorer, cruder empiricist attention. With the emphasis on the vertical reference they are looked at individually, assessed for their truth-bearing properties, and judged for their policy implications. As we have said, the emphasis in post 1974 research on seeking answers in appropriate places – the schoolrooms, the nurseries, the colleges – is profoundly to be welcomed, but it is insufficient.

The significance of studies comes, in our opinion, from their *horizontal* relationships, too seldom given their due in this country. The projects are items, getting meaning from their relationships to all the other items. Like words in a language their significance arises from their place in the structure as much as, or even more than, their reference to things, events or states of affairs. We offer an interpretation, which evaluates the trustworthiness of the different findings and judges their significance within a cautious quest for order, pattern and structure.

The book is, then, a reflection on the significance of various findings for the ways in which young children's education should be conducted. We shall be looking at a small, but for our purposes important, group of research initiatives and ideas and arguing our way through to some conclusions which, though necessarily interim and subjective, will have a reasonably legible signature.

CHAPTER 2
Schools and Teachers

In our view teachers frequently mistake short-term interest on the part of parents for long term confidence and fidelity. We think it would be timely for the whole of the profession to regard itself as client-centred. This doesn't mean that it should reflect faithfully the views of families any more than doctors do. It does mean that in the last analysis it is tried at the bar of public judgment.

Links with public authorities are much weaker than they once were and schools must work at relationships with their neighbourhoods. Home-school relations are still in their infancy in this country and as schools find it increasingly difficult to maintain relationships with their paymasters they must develop new trust and agreement with local families. Meantime, they are held responsible by the public and by government for what they achieve, and it clearly behoves teachers to reappraise the quality of what they offer.

Schools are parts of wider structures. They are subject to economic, social, cultural and political pressures and although they have control over only their internal organization, that has to be managed with due concern for the wider context. Nowhere is this more evident than the curriculum. Once considered the preserve of the school, it now belongs to the nation as a whole. In our view this applies as much to the nursery age as to school age children. Whether they are explicit or not the National Curriculum has aims. They indicate directions of learning with which for children's sakes teachers should comply. What children learn at school has to be within parental expectations which in turn are framed by decisions at national level.

Now, parents are entitled to expect that state schools will comply broadly with the National Curriculum guidelines. Thus teachers work within a framework which imposes obligations of both prudential and civic kinds. The former enjoins teachers to consider their professional contractual obligations to parents while the latter appeals to their positions as office holders within a democratic system.

Some may argue that it is ridiculous to invoke the National Curriculum for three-, four-, five- and six-year-olds. There is nothing in the national framework which requires separate subject categories at five and six years and much that indicates that official curriculum objectives can help to give direction to the schemes and webs designed for the younger pupils. Of course, as one moves from the junior/infant to the nursery curriculum, it is progressively more difficult to categorize activities under fields of knowledge but that is as it should be. All that is necessary is that schools can justify the activities they encourage as being compatible with, if not directly contributory to, the National Curriculum and show that they are successful educationally.

Whole school philosophy and policies

The philosophy and policies of whole school structures affect everyone and everything in the organization, including both classroom and tutorial contexts. For teachers to opt out of determining that structure and to give up responsibility for it is, we think, unethical. Correspondingly, we hold that headteachers have obligations to enable teaching staff (and other workers) to share decision taking and policy formation. While true collegiality of the sort urged by Campbell, Southworth and others may be impracticable or indeed undesirable it is imperative that staff contribute to and, within limits, uphold the policies of their schools.

We say 'within limits' because it would be a very 'organizational' form of ethics to insist that others toe the line on policies which they think are wrong. It seems to us that if the objections are overwhelmingly prudential then compliance should be expected; if they are, on the other hand, clearly moral then there could be a case for non compliance. We have in mind policies affecting ethnic customs or preferences, of which there are, regrettably, far too many examples. If it could be shown that such moral objections comply with the philosophical principles of the school, then there would of course be constitutional weight to them. This is why we emphasized both philosophy and policies. In any wholeschool structure they must both be accorded importance.

Philosophical principles are often criticized for being abstract and theoretical, timeless or lacking relevance. Staff sometimes feel it is a waste of time to bother about things that are so highfalutin, especially when circumstances demand action. Certainly, many of the aims and philosophies we have read are so lacking in depth and strength that it is quite clear that they have not been debated and examined. The only function they perform is to dress up the school brochure.

But without a school philosophy to appeal to, arguments against policies lack certain kinds of grounds. If there is a philosophy to which all agree then there is a powerful and constant body of principles against which certain aspects of policies can be measured. To introduce a quaint Victorian expression: everyone and everything has a besetting sin. If so, the besetting sin of policy is surely expediency. Policies are for meeting challenges, dealing with difficulties, smoothing out management, and so on. Admissions policies, behaviour policies, assembly policies, policies about dress, manners, sanctions: each of these *could* have moral implications. The philosophy of a school can act as a sort of ethical constitution. If we are really committed to providing for all, then should we be turning away an ethnic group, whether Christian, Muslim, traveller, or children with disabilities whether emotional, mental or physical? If we really believe that the religious beliefs of children within a school should be equally respected, how do we justify the celebration of some rather than other religious festivals?

We are not suggesting that the implications of the school philosophy ought to prevail against possible policies: we are saying that without principles to which people contribute and subscribe, and which they review, from time to time, against tough test cases, schools' inner dialogues are simply tactical and opportunist and no-one should be surprised if they deteriorate into merely functional businesses. But a whole school philosophy should provide more than an ethical dimension. It should be clear about its religious orientation. To many parents religious culture is of major importance in their children's development and they are entitled to know where a school stands. For many schools the wider structures in which they are situated limit their freedom to decide for themselves. Decisions by the State, or membership of a Church, or location within an ethnically close-knit community have implications for schools which it would be absurd to ignore. Nevertheless, if there are not decisions of kind to make there will be choices of emphasis and degrees of toleration.

The third major dimension of the school philosophy is the pedagogical – its perspective on teaching and learning. Leaving aside the
broad framework of learning which a State school is expected to offer and for which it is held accountable, there are decisions of importance to be made. The National Curriculum contains assumptions
about the classification of knowledge into subject areas. At various
points in their school lives pupils will be tested in accordance with
those classifications. What view does the school take of the framing
of knowledge? What view does it take of what knowledge is? It seems
to us that how a school decides to organize knowledge for teaching
purposes depends on its answers to such questions.

We take a structural perspective on knowledge. We look at its
vertical references and at its horizontal significance. On the former
we would say knowledge differs from belief in at least one essential
respect: a claim has passed certain truth tests and is held to be, if
only temporarily, reasonably trustworthy. We would go somewhat
further along this vertical reference and say that in order to credit
children with knowing something that we count as true we should
want from them some reasonable account of why they are confident
it should be trusted.

As for the horizontal significance, we cannot make any sense of an
item unless we can locate it within a network of related items. We say
that of anything, whether it is a thing or a proposition. Groupings are
all-important. Without them how can anything be understood, or be
given appropriate consideration? Of course, one arrangement can
obscure another, which is a good reason for avoiding rigidity in organizing knowledge. But knowledge without the grouping of items
simply does not make sense. One does not have to be a student of
Levi-Strauss to appreciate the importance of lists for connotations of
meaning, nor a follower of Umberto Eco to see the importance of
library classifications for locating knowledge. That the memory of an
emotional event can be triggered years later and disorganize and
incapacitate someone may, when classified under psychology, help
in our understanding of memory; under criminology it could lead us
to the motivation for a brutal slaying. What we should be aiming
for in children is the development of the ability to categorize and
recategorize so that different perspectives can be opened up.

The teachers' work of developing children's understanding is essentially about helping them to making sense of the world by recognizing important and accessible patterns, by applying analytic tools
of doubt and test, by imagining things to be otherwise than they seem

to be, by sharing emotions and friendships. The school should aim at laying down trustworthy foundations for later learning and unlearning. For us, this is, in the last analysis, an individual affair.

In saying that the school pedagogic philosophy is ultimately about each child's development, we are saying nothing about general patterns of teaching. What it does commit us to is attention to the thinking of individual children. Research at Exeter University has been particularly effective at showing how, in favourable circumstances, teachers can organize their work to make time to discuss with children how they get solutions to problems, thus breaking in to the process-chains of reasoning. There are good reasons for groups, but in the end it is individual attention that matters. We want to call this kind of teaching 'tutoring' and any pedagogic policies must make space for it.

Are there any principles that should take precedence over general patterns of teaching? We are at one with many, such as Katz and Sylva who emphasize the individual growth of autonomy as an aim, but we agree with Robson (1990) that there is no positive necessary connexion between the development of autonomy and particular classroom structures. As for teaching methods, in his *Paideia Program* (1984) Adler argued for a functional distinction between teaching methods, distinguishing three broad types: instructing, coaching and discussing. Educating children involves giving them new information and it would be unjustified to ignore instructive skills of clarifying, ordering and presenting. Learning involves demonstration and practice of skills and there is a considerable literature, especially from the sports world, about how to make exercise-tasks both enjoyable and effective, and how expert attention from someone who knows how to do it can make all the difference to children.

And then there is understanding. Embedded in knowledge and skills there are concepts and these need discussion in groups of reasonable size. Once again, there is considerable research evidence available on teaching by discussion. Adler's sharp philosophy of teaching has much to commend it. It needs supplementing, in our opinion, by self-denying ordinances on the part of teachers – by standing off, leaving room for spontaneity, allowing the idiosyncratic growth of ideas – but it cuts through much woolly thinking about teaching and reminds us that although some methods must be cast out on grounds of profanity, there is nothing so sacred that its suitability should not be justified. The difference between a whole school philosophy and a policy is that whereas the former provides a framework within which certain aspects of policies can be evaluated, the latter is a specific structure for dealing with certain sorts of decisions.

Schools can, and often do, function without policies but it is a practice without much general recommendation. Schools need managing and policies are rational instruments of planning, giving consistency of practice, establishing a history of decisions and allowing for critical discussion. The absence of policies does not entail the absence of decisions. Schools may, for instance, have time divisions, or space divisions which are as they are simply because they were as they were: nevertheless they continue to be sanctioned. The absence of a 'no' usually means 'yes'.

If there are no policies in a given area reflection is made difficult because, in the absence of a rational case for the distribution of time and space, questioning could be interpreted as challenge to whatever authority sanctioned it. Headteachers have been known to be sensitive to such vibrations.

It might be objected that the distribution of time and space is not normally the kind of thing about which policies are formed. The more usual subject would be handwriting or fighting or school uniform. However, these are the kinds of contexts in which we are interested. If the distribution is one teacher to a class, with helpers weighted towards the younger children, we want to ask: is this the outcome of a policy, are the reasons good enough, how beneficial are the total consequences, is there any incompatibility with the school philosophy?

The notion of collegiality is clearly relevant to policy making. It is usually taken to refer to an outcome: the sharing by staff of responsibility for the way the school runs. As to the basis on which staff should cooperate, there are many variations on perhaps two main models. One stresses *unity*, achieving teamwork, sense of corporate mission and a community spirit through a basic like-mindedness among the staff, without the need for a structure of rights; the other, *pluralism*, emphasizing basic structures of individual rights and rules of procedure which ensure that points of view are heard.

When there are like minded and enthusiastic teaching staff it is tempting to overlook the establishment of proper structures including agreed practices about meetings, minutes, resolutions, the dispersal of responsibilities, etc., but the advantage of such arrangements is that they establish a framework within which disagreement and even conflict can be managed. What is more, they can support staff who are not like-minded, who might, precisely because of their differences, produce better quality policy. Without such arrangements staffs of this kind could find themselves unable to cooperate.

It is probably clear from the tenor of the above that of the two we prefer a collegial set up based on well-defined and agreed procedures and rights. While freely admitting that it does not guarantee more effective operation – indeed, collegiality itself does not do that – it has advantages over the other in ensuring that voices are heard, power is dispersed, decisions are joint, and responsibility shared. The legislative body of the school has more chance of forming realistic and helpful policies if the very people affected by those policies are entitled to a say in the decision making process.

Pioneering work on collegiality has been undertaken by Holly Campbell, Southworth and Wallace, with valuable contributions by Coulson and Nias. Working with Southworth and Nias on the Primary School Staff Relationships Project (1989) Robin Yeomans has extended the notion to include the non-teaching staff. To what extent should they participate in collegiality? What are the issues – confidentiality, expertise, perhaps professional status?

We think the most important of the policy decisions are those to do with pedagogy, that is to say, teaching and learning. We take that to be the main point of the school's existence. As we have already discussed, we believe the broad outlines of the state school curriculum are given within larger structures than that of the individual State school. However this does not absolve a school from a number of policy decisions. These will include at least the following: the progressive differentiation of the curriculum, involving stronger framing by teachers of older children; the analysis, planning and sequencing of topics; the designation of specialist working areas, and arrangements for assessment and recording.

Pedagogical policies will need to address the arrangements for children of markedly differing abilities, specialist teaching, material provision, parental help, the timetable, management of time in classrooms, and so on. It should not be forgotten, either, that in the first school the policy on assemblies is of major importance: their timing, duration, character and purpose affect the whole school (see McCreery, 1991). If teachers are not involved in such policies, powers of decision with regard to their own classrooms may be severely restricted.

Classroom philosophy and arrangements

Classroom arrangements are, within the constraints of school policies, and consistent with school philosophy, the particular responsibility of class teachers. It is they who have to lay down and maintain the conditions in which their class communities live and work. They decide how decisions are made and by whom; by their decrees and by their omissions so should they be judged. Nursery or classroom communities are developed and presided over by teachers. The rules, the values, the expectations, the standards are all for them to decide. Save for a few constraints and problems of implementation or maintenance they are the authorities for these structures and must shoulder the responsibilities.

Our view is that the structure at class or nursery room level should again involve two interacting elements: a philosophy and 'arrangements'. At a basic level a teacher is responsible for the progress and well-being of a group of children. To some extent the philosophy and policies for the whole school will require conformity from the class teacher but in the last analysis he or she is a particular individual and the class a particular grouping of children. There should be an underlying rationale for the class. Its principles should, in theory if not wholly in practice, be understood and subscribed to by the children; if possible children should be involved drawing it up.

Children are affected by the community philosophy in which they spend their school day. This does not merely impose external constraints upon what they may or may not do, but shapes their development in both rational and affective ways. The philosophy underlying their community life should be justifiable to them, should they be in a position to query it; alterable by them if they have the power to advance good reasons for its modification and, above all, open to their developing powers of perception.

It will also be a shaping agent in their own moral development. The paths to developing moral maturity may be impossible to discern for older children but for the ages we address in this book the elements of moral development are surely clear. Children need to acquire the reasoning skills and structures to come to moral judgments. They have to be able to take into account both forward-looking aspects of actions, such as their consequences for good or bad, and the backward-looking conceptions, such as promises, loyalties, responsibilities and rights. The influence of the classroom philosophy is inescapably part of this developmental task.

Then they must be capable of a range of feelings and emotions. Developing that capacity involves, in our view, raising and tapping feelings, extending the palette of responses, and guiding them towards appropriate affective relationships, such as pity for victims, anger at injustice, magnanimity for the defeated. As well as sympathy, empathy ought to be an objective. Having sympathy for someone who is racially abused may not help one to know what it feels like to be patronised. Role changing in a supportive community can help.

In character training – for that is what, we suppose, we are talking about – children have to be assisted to deal with temptation. It is not just young children who get seduced by fair prospects or deflected from duty by inconvenience. Lastly, they should come to know and be sustained by a range of consistently applied values which will help them to make moral sense of their lives. All this important development will benefit from a growing awareness of the values which underlie approved classroom relationships.

Classroom philosophy differs from the school version. The latter is more debatable: there are adults, there are rival claims. It can be represented in words. Classroom philosophy is, at best, an attempt at representing in words something which is like a complex seedbed of values, indispensable to the ecosystem of the classroom. It can never be fully known by the teacher because the teacher is a part of it. But if the elucidation of the value system of the classroom is resistant to all except skilled ethnographers, the curricular and pedagogic dimensions of the classroom philosophy should be explicable. School policies will set certain parameters but within those the teachers should be clear about what aims and conditions they want to achieve.

Willig (1990) takes a straightforward view of classroom knowledge arguing that so long as the teacher is clear about the advantages of organizing learning in terms of disciplines there is no necessary reason for children, particularly young children, to see things in that way. At the same time, however, he points out that there is some evidence to show that children, like adults, seem to learn better when they see the point of something, or when they see its connection with something their parents see the point of.

Our point in referring to Willig's view is that we think it is important to have a sense of what one is educating children into. In this case it is structures of knowledge which will not only empower children to find out more, because they contain methods and attitudes of mind as well as networks of related concepts, but link in important and well-tried ways with still finer differentiations of knowledge. Thus children will not be sidelined by what they learn, or left with unconnected episodes of bliss.

We take the view that young children are themselves the starting points for the work that is undertaken. At the beginning of the year, although teachers have a rough idea of the general levels of achievement they expect children to reach by the end of the year, they do not know what the children know, nor do they know what the children misunderstand.Much of the work would then be exploratory on the part of the teachers. Bennett and his co-researchers found in their 1984 study that match was greatest in the first term as teachers attentively assessed their children's interests and capabilities. We should seek ways of extending that period.

But such attention is costly in terms of time. How might time be saved? In the same project Bennett came to similar conclusions to Doyle in the States. Their preferred teaching style (albeit for the older children of our range) was to see classes as comprising several groups. With clear instructions from teachers, relevant information properly displayed and materials to hand, groups could take responsibility for interpreting teacher intentions and through internal discussion develop their problem-solving activities.

The idea is to release teachers from nagging questions and requests so that they have time to observe and analyse, judging when information and demonstration are needed, when errors are being committed, when group dynamics need modification, and when individual groups are ready to report. In the final analysis the teachers need to make space for effective tutorial relationships. Such a classroom philosophy is by no means complete but it can act as a criteriological framework for assessing the arrangements made by the teacher. The sooner children are in a position to contribute to the formulation and modification of these the better, it is a measure of their development. The arrangements themselves will depend on the age of the children.

For the age group we are mainly concerned with however – three to six – the arrangements should relate to human rather than academic ends. By this we mean that there is so much unenforced spontaneous learning going on that the focus should be the children – as individuals, as groups and as the total classroom community. Because many will be away from the family and possibly a whole culture for the first time, identity, a feeling of being special, of being oneself, and a feeling of belonging to larger structures are very important. We think that identity is associated with an address and therefore the allocation of a classroom space is essential.

There has been much work on the idea of structuring the environment and structuring the day. As we shall be arguing later, we think that many commentators want to go much further than we in the direction of pinning children down to activities and times; nevertheless we do think routines are important. Similarly, although we think material provision in the form of fixed, well-differentiated areas within the nursery and reception class tradition is significant, we do not, as we shall again explain later, on the whole approve of designating areas by what activities should go on there. Activities should be created which groups or single children can accomplish. Classically they should be designed to incorporate curriculum objectives within schemes which are clear to the teacher and matched to children's interests and abilities. Out of the many studies on match we have, as we mentioned before, gained most benefit from those of Doyle working out of Austin, Texas.

He draws attention to the sheer complexity of the subject, contrasting assumptions about difficulty or levels in number work with those in literature or games. Of course the very act of devising task activities itself involves not only diagnosis of ability and interest but judgments about how to meet them. Should one match ability, aim higher, set out to puzzle?

Meadows and Cashdan (*Helping Children Learn*, 1988) refer, as many others do, to Vygotsky's notion that we should think of children as being at two levels of development. One is the level of their present operation and the other is the level they could reach with some help. With this notion Vygotsky shows the limitations of the Piagetian approach for the teacher. The 'two levels' idea requires teachers to make that upper level accessible so that children can accomplish tasks that would be beyond their level one competence. 'Teaching that is directed towards getting children to do *without* help what they can at present do only *with* help is the best way to improve development (1988, p.53).

Activities are many and various. There is a demonstration of some kind, an introduction to a new area which could herald the activities, and correspondingly an interested appreciation of children's explorations and accomplishments. There is the whole class discussion which provides the opportunity for sharing stories and news and its

18

transformation into a kind of moot for judgments about behaviour and events. There is the solitary practice of skills – handwriting, modelling, balancing. There is opportunity for free exploration. And there is the large corporate activity such as a play or team game. Overall, the day should have a sort of unity and offer the teacher ample opportunity for close observation of the children so that his or her work can continue to extend their interests and capabilities.

Tutorial philosophy and tutorial contexts

We regard tutorial relationships as really the whole point of schools. School policies and classroom arrangements provide the conditions for the observed growth of learning but tutorials provide individual attention.

Once discussions about *educare* and *educere* were common and led to fruitful speculation, especially by Richard Peters (1966). It is no longer fashionable to turn to etymology to ascertain current meaning but we derive some pleasure from noting the origin of the word 'tutor'. Our dictionary gives us the Latin *tutela* meaning 'a watching'. Tutelage is the state of being under a guardian or tutor. For us, tutorials connote watchful attention. They demand from the tutors quiet, still action. It is pupils who perform; tutors assess and intervene. Pupils display the state of their learning and their tutors the arts of sensitive criticism.

The philosophy or rationale of the tutorial can be related to the Bennett study referred to earlier, in which he gives many examples of mistakes children make when doing arithmetic or writing. Where children are asked to explain how they get to their answers, they frequently tangle or elide elements of their reasoning or show misunderstanding of some fundamental concept. Of course the tutorial does not only only detect and rectify error, it celebrates progress and mastery and serves as significant feedback to children. It is indispensable to really good teaching and all teachers should make time for such tutorial activity. The contexts for the expression of this philosophy are many and varied. There seem to us no necessary conditions, whether of silence or privacy. Children rapidly appreciate when an exchange is professionally ringfenced and respect the fact. Sometimes, of course, privacy of a sort is important, when loss of face is a significant factor, but that is likely to be seldom at the age we address. These then are the tutorial contexts – those frameworks of interaction between teachers and children which are most intensely related to learning – the teaching relationships in which puzzlement is expressed, alternative explanations considered and ideas formulated.

Again, it seems important to us that the principles which inform the tutorials contexts should cohere in some way with those of the classroom and the whole school. They are the epicentres, the central structures in which teachers help children to make better sense of things. And because aiding them to understand involves patient listening and watching so that diagnosis of errors of fact and logic may be identified, the tutorial relationships are not always under teacher control. Inescapable, however, is the professional responsibility. At the heart of teaching is ethics.

Tutorial contexts are not entirely up to tutors. They can do so much, but at this sharp end of teaching they are constrained by the necessity to watch, listen and analyse. Importantly for tutoring purposes, as distinct from reassuring or bonding purposes, they have to break into the thinking chains, to see how children get to the conclusions they do, a process that has more than a little in common with student supervision. And as in that practice it has to be done with encouragement.

The teacher

We approach the complex idea of a teacher from two perspectives: epistemological and ethical. The first emphasizes the quality of a teacher's thinking about knowledge; the second the ethical quality of his or her thinking about educating children and what it involves.

The epistemological perspective: thinking about knowledge

That teachers are specialists in knowledge is an often heard but puzzling claim. Most teachers would, for example, fasten on the word 'specialist' and divide themselves into those who concentrate on a particular subject and those who see themselves as generalists. Usually generalists are found more in evidence among the teachers of younger children. Since our topic is the education of young children the attitude their teachers take to knowledge is of some concern to us.

There are at least two ways in which the word 'generalist' can be taken. One is that the teachers specialize in 'general knowledge', interpreted as a kind of everyday know-how, with perhaps an emphasis on practical knowledge and common sense. Their justification for thus specializing is that it is sufficient for young children. If pressed, these teachers may well go beyond that to the claim that they are not there to teach knowledge at all, but to teach children. If that is meant literally then of course the response is, what is it you are going to teach them? That the answer must in some form or another refer to knowledge is obvious. But it might be a more sophisticated point than that. The teachers might be emphasizing that their role is to assist the growth of understanding in children and that what is relevant to that is not curricular knowledge but knowledge of child development.

We are somewhat dubious about this. There seems to be a view that in some way understanding of child development has come snowballing down through the traditions of nursery and infant education gathering size, weight and authority as it nears the present. But close reading of the theory and practice of teaching young children does not yield evidence which would support it. Rousseau, Pestalozzi, Herbart, Owen, Froebel, the McMillans, Steiner, Montessori, Susan Isaacs, Anna Freud present to readers a bewildering contrast of ideas, so much so that the onus is surely on those who claim to see consistency to demonstrate it.

And if one turns from the early childhood education tradition to the contemporary study of child development there is even less prospect of a unified theory. Modern psychologists are as involved in the tumult of theory and counter-theory as other scientists are. The undoubted fact that there is research of the highest class devoted to the finding and establishing of child development principles seems for some people to be sufficient grounds for the belief that trustworthy principles have been agreed.

Any developmental theory has to account for typical patterns of change between two points, whether they are acorns and oaks, tadpoles and frogs or babies and mature adults. Once such patterns of physical growth between babies and mature adults have been established, the theories which purport to explain them are testable against experience and replaceable by more and more sophisticated accounts as scientists build up their knowledge. As a result of such work we know certain things about the rapid growth of young infants up to the age of three or four and the much slower, more regular, growth up to puberty.

Nevertheless, it is objected, cognitive development is surely indispensable: it underpins all our professional understanding of young children. If nothing else remains, cognitive development must. Well... must it? Formerly the theories of Jean Piaget were the subject of strong claims in teacher education. Even now a quiet conviction persists that although we must acknowledge modifications of his theories they provide the underlying explanations of how young children develop in their thinking.

But the modifications are so significant that there are grounds for questioning whether Piaget is taught in anything but name any more. Furthermore there are rival and conflicting modifications. And as if that were not enough, there are whole perspectives on cognitive learning which challenge the Piagetian. So where are these uncontroversial but illuminating 'principles of cognitive development'? What there is, in our view, is a veritable snakepit of contesting hypotheses. Intellectually exciting no doubt, and doubtless of interest to reflective teachers. But, apart from near-tautologies, there is no certainty: no dependable principles smoothly derived from some well-shaped and thoroughly checked out theory.

So, when we hear that teachers know, or should be taught 'the principles of child development' we get extremely worried. We not only don't believe the principles of child development have been discovered, we don't think they can be discovered. Moreover, even if they were discovered, we don't believe we or anyone else would or could know that they were the principles. Uncertainty is built into knowledge; that is why the quality of judgment is so important and reflectiveness so prized.

We quite accept, of course, that the study of human development is a legitimate and important area for research; that researchers frequently produce work that is relevant and interesting to teachers; that developmental psychologists and teachers have fields of attention which overlap, but just as there are many kinds of teacher and things which they do, so too are there many developmental psychologists. Only those who suppose Pestalozzi and Froebel thought alike about children's education will suppose that the work of Piaget and Bruner is of a piece. Indeed Piaget and Bruner would be the first to say that there are many Piagets and Bruners. It is all a far cry from the idea of a unified body of knowledge from which uncontested principles for teaching syllogistically flow.

Guiding the learning of young children benefits from both child development theory and from careful planning in which teachers know what they are counting as progress points and when individual children reach them. It requires thought about classroom frameworks in which curriculum objectives and a range of teaching methods and grouping options for implementing them are clear to the teacher. And the classroom strategies should fit in with the overall curricular and pedagogical philosophy of the school.

We cannot help structuring environments for children; what matters is the quality of what we do. This is not an arcane matter. We don't have to learn a new vocabulary for it. There are principles underlying such activities but they are not like conclusions to syllogisms. Teachers should study teachers and children interacting. The actual contexts of teaching – the classroom, the nurseries, the playgrounds and the home – are the appropriate targets of study.

Earlier we said that there were at least two senses in which a teacher of young children might claim to be a generalist in knowledge. Having discussed one we now address the other. Again it contrasts with the idea of a subject specialist. This time, however, it concedes nothing epistemologically. Whereas specialists would know a given area very thoroughly in terms of its key concepts, its truth tests and its characteristic methodologies; whereas they could trace relations between the specialist area and its neighbours, generalists would chart several areas using essentially the same distinctions.

We referred to one Victorian phrase earlier in the book, here we recall another: the Golden Circle of Knowledge. This diagram represented all the forms of knowledge savants were presumed to know. For us, generalist teachers in the second sense of the term would attend to such a totality; would be alive to essential differences and shadings between important areas. This is of paramount importance in the nursery classroom where individual paths of learning have to be located and interpreted by teachers responsible for guiding children's overall understanding.

For primary school teachers it seems clear at last that neither a piecemeal, strongly framed, divisive approach to subjects nor the project-and-topic dominated programme will optimally help children to make sense of the world. There are strengths and weaknesses in both the discipline and topic based curricula, as Richard Pring has convincingly argued over a long period, but it has taken radical changes in what is asked of schools for the general realization to take place. With regard to the curriculum of the youngest children, we are well aware of UK teachers' wariness of attempts to impose a programme 'from above', but we have no sympathy with the view that there should be no curriculum at all. It is a logical nonsense since successful teaching implies learning, and learning implies the development of skills and understanding or – to put it another way – the growth of practical and theoretical knowledge. It also implies a kind of false consciousness because teachers are, whether they admit it to themselves or not, providing a curriculum by the things they do or do not encourage and permit. Joan Tamburrini (1981, p.161) put it succinctly:

> Possibly the most dangerous misconception is the idea that a curriculum can be neutral... It is constructed by people with ideas about what is desirable and undesirable in the educational process and these ideas are reflected both wittingly and unwittingly in the curriculum and thence in what the children do.

The 'webbing' so common in the UK for mapping out curricula for young children, where teachers take the interests and experiences of children and contextualize them in loose maps of curriculum objectives related to later curriculum developments, has much to commend it. It is, however, neither necessary nor sufficient for good curriculum planning. It is not necessary because other approaches are available and may be suited to particular circumstances. And it is not sufficient because it does not automatically demand from teachers either reasonably clear ideas on what learning should be encouraged, or the appreciation of important distinctions over widely differing areas of knowledge. Our point in emphasizing the importance of the generalist is that, with sensitive understanding of young children and their interests, such a teacher would be able to use the webbing tool, or any other, effectively.

The ethical perspective: being a teacher

This brings us to the last part of this section: the ethics of the teacher. Much has been written about this subject, particularly in the USA. Brubacher's now dated famous chapter in his *Modern Philosophies of Education* (1962), 'Professional Ethics' focuses on the behaviour of the teacher within a status matrix. We see, for example, the injunction against a teacher applying for position which is not yet vacant. To do so would undermine, we are told, relationships between members of the profession and weaken that high ethical resolve which runs through all of a professional's relationships with fellow professionals and clients. Recalling this chapter underlines the mercilessness with which changing contexts deal with pronouncements about what is and what is not 'done'.

More recently Passmore (1984) fastens on a professional duty. Taking duties to be correlative of rights he argues that because teachers have privileged knowledge about students they are under obligations of confidentiality. If isolated individuals were to break such trusts there would have to be some way that the profession could mete out punishment. The alternative would be to do nothing, which would amount to the condoning of such behaviour, and that could have only one outcome: the withdrawal of privileged information and the reduction of the teaching profession to functionaries. Passmore calls for a sustained examination of teachers' professional ethics.

At Teacher's College New York, in his sharply conceived series on school ethics, Jonas Soltis and his team of writers explored such territory with a series of case studies on teaching and school administration. Though largely single issue problems, they have the potential for developing rich human complexities. The cases nearly always arise from that region where personal freedom and professional obligation interrelate and have through their vivid realization an immediate impact which will last until the particular circumstances they invoke become timeworn.

When we write of teacher ethics or professional ethics none of these approaches quite answers what we are getting at and we refer to them in order to clarify the outlines of our own view. The important phrases in our introduction to this section on the teacher are *thinking about knowledge* and *ethical quality of his or her thinking about educating children*. There is a sense of 'outer' and 'inner' here. The first phrase has the sense of an accomplishment about it, the second refers to a person's nature or being. In writing of the ethics of teachers we have in mind their values: what they think of as important.

How a person behaves towards pupils or colleagues or the public is, within certain limits, beside the point. A great many books emphasize social attitudes or public standards or institutional norms as measures for how people should re-present themselves in their roles as teachers. Books on management urge certain forms of behaviour, particularly interpersonal behaviour, as conduct to be aimed at, as if they were somehow high up in a hierarchy of teacher quality ratings rather than functionally correct organizational virtues. But many of the most acclaimed teachers of the past would not last five minutes in most model teams of modern management. How would Pestalozzi or Froebel 'fit in'? Teaching has been an ill-starred profession for many of those most committed to it. Parental unease and official disapproval have seen to that. Even fellow teachers have not been reluctant to denounce and expel.

Of course, a balance has to be struck. Parents are right to have reservations about entrusting their children to schools and teachers. It should go without saying. But if there are two clear views for teachers in this book, they are:

(i) that their structures should be 'loose enough' to let children experiment, make errors and pursue unplanned for trails and

(ii) that norms should have high toleration so that temperament, interests and behaviour – in short, children's 'nature' – should not be constrained within too narrow limits.

Our view is that administrators too should bear them in mind for their staff. It is a rather stronger interpretation of respect for persons than is usually put forward, entailing a stronger version of privacy. Yet we underline it.

Jennifer Nias (1989) and Stephen Ball and Ivor Goodson (1985) have drawn attention to the astonishing variety of motivations different teachers have. Carey Bennett, writing in the latter, acutely draws attention to the perspectives of art teachers to the schools in which they work, finding satisfactions and irritations that colleagues do not even dream of. Should a staff accommodate William Blake? Many of the best teachers relate more easily to children or to their subjects than to fellow professionals. They may deplore or fret at giving time to formfilling and returns, or 'rendering account' to non-specialists. They may miss meetings, or behave unhelpfully when they attend. But if they are outstanding teachers, they should, within reasonable limits, be accommodated. Teaching is a creative activity as well as a methodical one. Nietzsche's warning that the spirit of Dionysus is at least as important as that of Apollo applies to teaching just as much as to art, perhaps even more so.

We are not claiming that such people are models for, or typical of, the teaching profession. We are saying that their intensity will often reveal features of personal educational philosophy which we should learn to recognize in the less extreme displays of more run of the mill members of the profession, and thus pay more heed to what is intrinsic to a teacher's outlook than to what corresponds to the prevailing public or institutional expectations. What sorts of features? We would pick out three: (i) a respect for pupils; (ii) a care for the effects of teacher influence on pupils and (iii) a concern about the quality of teaching.

(i) Respect for pupils. We use the word 'pupils' rather than 'children' for a particular reason. Within the European early childhood tradition there has been an idealization of the child. In recent times Ronald King in *All Things Bright and Beautiful* and the more recent *Informality, Ideology and Infants' schooling* (1988) has drawn attention to the persistence of this tendency but it was of concern to Susan Isaacs too. Her first biographer, Dorothy Gardner, contrasted her approach to that of Froebel:

> He tended, as Rousseau did, to idealize them. He was, therefore, unaware, as Susan so vividly *was* aware, of the need to permit and provide for sublimatory outlets for feelings of hate and aggression. Susan brought a much more objective and biological approach to her observations of children, and had respect for the real child's own wishes and feelings. Dr Edna Oakshott wrote: 'Through the able exposition of her findings, the mystical approach to children, which had been for so long an obstacle to sound educational theory, was successfully challenged and the young child was brought into the perspective of human growth.' (Susan Isaacs, 1969, pp.162-3)

We prefer 'pupils' because it signifies that children are already in a role relationship with teachers, whose purpose it is to influence and affect pupils. There is therefore no question of the agonising which sometimes accompanies child-centred educational theory; rather, it is a matter of defining limits to teacher influence. As Margaret Brett (1991) has recently argued: as opposed to idealization of children, respect for pupils positively demands intervention from teachers, on the grounds that children are learning indiscriminately, extramurally, all the time they are learning in school. The limits we would advocate are similar to those of Susan Isaacs' Malting House School. Quoting from notes made by a member of staff, Evelyn Lawrence, Gardner writes:

> They must have intellectual curiosity and vigour, and be averse to taking their opinions ready-made. They must also be as physically

healthy as is possible. I think this is as far as Dr Isaacs would go in particularization.' (Ibid, p.61)

(ii) Care for the effects on pupils. Is the provision rich, relevant to the pupils' interests, and broad? Is the observation acute and sustained? Is the information given to the pupils true, right, stimulating? Is the pupil better able to cope with things in general? And is the pupil growing as an individual in his or her own right? Teachers should not forget that their impact is incalculable. Long after their names and personalities have been forgotten, something of them may live on in their pupils.

(iii) Concern about the quality of teaching. Teachers should be reflectively concerned about the quality of their teaching. In his work on the teaching of subjects like music and architecture Donald Schon has brought into professional consciousness the essentially creative nature of teaching. It demands, he says, a continual reflection-in-action as the very terms in which teachers construe their professional work need constant modification and updating. In their commentary on Schon, Bullough, Knowles and Crow (1991, p.82) point out that teachers make use of frameworks within which they attend to features which are often of their own making. They maintain that the problems which teachers select to deal with are often self-constructed and teachers, just as much as young children do, need to de-centre. Schon is, of course, making another point too: teaching needs pupils; its quality can therefore never be guaranteed in advance.

CHAPTER 3
Early Childhood Education

Noting that the 'English Nursery School' was a phrase which was widely used abroad, Lesley Webb studied the development of the nursery movement since the turn of the century in an effort to discover the substance behind the expression. She concluded that there seemed to be three main elements: health, socialization, and the encouragement of curiosity, experiment, constructive skills and creative abilities. She argued that none of them had 'been given analytic treatment of a thoroughly convincing kind' (1974, p.4).

More recently Tina Bruce (1987) looked at what she similarly described as the 'common law' of the early childhood tradition. She too noted the agreement of teachers but found it superficial. Her plan was to acknowledge frankly the confusion which underlay the consensus and attempt to find a pattern to serve as a trustworthy rationale for working with young children. Rejecting what she termed nativism and empiricism she held that underlying the differences between such pioneers as Froebel, Montessori and Steiner there was a consistent belief in the interactionist approach. She drew out ten principles which should in her opinion underpin contemporary practice.

From a different stance again, Van der Eyken (1986) wrote of an 'unspoken but implied consensus' (p.1). It was all the more remarkable because the range of institutions which served young children was so wide and sprang from such different origins. Drawing on his own surveys of pre-school provision he established that there was an extraordinary commonality of provision among the thousands of different institutions. Painting, sand and water play were available 'most of every session' in 98% of hall-based playgroups, while 76% had fantasy play regularly on offer. It should be borne in mind that his was quantitative research, and such categories are bound to include large variations in actual provision. He commented that he feared that many pre-school programmes were designed to be 'occupying' rather than directly stimulating, reflecting the 'now-familiar provision that transcends all under-five provision' (p.7). He went on to agree with both Webb and Bruce in his conclusion:

> I hope I have made my case that we need to re-think the curriculum, both its content and the way in which it is presented; building on the past, certainly, but not slavishly following a faded model. (p.14).

As a researcher of the Malting House School with its fierce scientific emphasis he was also puzzled by the ubiquitous preference for 'ludic' over 'epistemic' play. The distinction, explored systematically by Corinne Hutt in a number of articles, refers to play which stresses the fantasy element, including dolls, home corner, painting, sand and water, as opposed to play concerned with learning skills or acquiring knowledge, including construction toys, books, cutting and sticking puzzles. While there are aspects of this distinction needing further discussion, it is undeniable that the emphasis on ludic play is remarkable.

In speculating why it came about, Van der Eyken reflected on the nursery tradition. Unlike Bruce he placed Froebel and Montessori quite apart, suggesting that when Montessori's approach and materials became known in the 1920s it was a challenge to the Froebelian method. The innovation did not however become popular, he said, because at about the same time 'England had become the refugee home of another, new, school of thought: psychoanalysis' (p.9).

He traced strong connexions between Melanie Klein and Susan Isaacs who was involved in psychoanalysis at the time Klein first lectured in England. Klein's pioneering work on 'play-technique' was used at the Malting House School in its short but influential existence. On its close Isaacs renewed her psychoanalytic training and in 1933 became Head of the new Department of Child Development at the University of London Institute of Education. Although much of her influence stemmed from her pioneering work at the Malting house, subsequently recorded in her writings, she was, as Gammage reports (1986, p.17) enormously influential in her new post. Van der Eyken concluded that the concern for the child's psychological state, self-expression, and so on, which was so prominent a feature of the Cambridge school, was propagated by Isaacs and her disciples.

Both Van der Eyken and Gammage make the same point: what actually went on at The Malting House was both infinitely richer and more complex than the influences it has had. At Malting House the play-technique element was secondary to an overriding concern with children's active enquiry. Here the 'scientific method' was employed to the degree that 'one had to live with the consequences of one's actions'. Faced with the results of his surveys he asked: 'But where is 'active enquiry' in pre-schooling today ... Where, indeed, is the outside world?' (p.12).

In outlining in some detail certain aspects of the nursery tradition it is intended to demonstrate that the process by which it has formed a 'common law' has not aided progress, in spite of the fact that many of the influences upon it seem, intuitively at least, to be very sound. For instance, using Susan Isaacs as one example, it seems that apart from isolated cases the general practical application is a weak version, a watered down interpretation of prescriptive theory.

We maintain that to the three elements of received opinion, practical experience and prescriptive theory, it is important that the findings of systematic research are applied. Whilst it was a construct of those elements which formed the nursery tradition in the first place, that construct was not a product of critical analysis. Instead, it seems to have evolved through an interweaving of these elements, sometimes harmoniously, sometimes as the result of bitter polemics. Unfortunately, while neither harmony nor rivalry alone is necessarily detrimental to criticism, the interaction of the two is potentially hostile to analysis and evidence. The 'common law' appears to have been compacted to a lowest common denominator, a baseline provision, which is, paradoxically, honoured again and again. This might in part owe something to a lack of critical training, compounded over the years by incoming influences that are improperly reviewed or simply stitched together and result in conceptual confusion.

The 1988 Report of the House of Commons *Education, Science and Arts Committee on Education Provision for the Under Fives* exemplifies the features of the 'common law' of the early childhood tradition. How much like previous statements is the Committee's definitive statement of quality (paragraph 51, p.xx-xxi):

... the aim of early education was to meet the child's intellectual aesthetic, emotional, physical and social development. A variety of needs which a child has in the course of this development were drawn to our attention in the evidence submitted. Young children need to be with adults who are interested and interesting, and with other children to whom they may relate. They need to have natural objects and artefacts to handle and explore. They need opportunity to communicate through music and imaginative play and they require space and opportunity for physical activities. These needs can only be met if an appropriate environment is provided with adults who understand something of child development and are ready and able to listen, encourage and stimulate.

Detailing much that is generally and perhaps properly valued by practitioners it is, nevertheless, disappointing in its reluctance to take a fresh look at the 'inheritance' at a time when it is apparently fairly well placed to do so.

It is also peppered with 'needs' and clearly embedded in assumptions of a social compensatory kind. In considering the value of the concept of need Woodhead (1987) helps to highlight the inadequacy of such a statement, pointing out that not only must reference to needs become less simplistic as we understand more about human development, but also that we must, in identifying needs:

Make personal and professional value judgments about what are the desirable childhood experiences in relation to the cultural context into which they are growing up.It also depends crucially on reconciling the various goals for children's development to those responsible for promoting it, including parents and teachers as well as politicians and child welfare professionals. (p.137).

The element that is missing in the common law tradition is knowledge about just what goes on in nursery classrooms. We have accounts of rare experimental classes and impressions of mainstream classes but there is nothing to compare with the growing descriptive research of today. We are indeed fortunate that we are starting to build up a theoretical knowledge with which we can once again begin to interrogate the rich nursery tradition. It is our hope that the work of the early pioneers, both famous and at present unknown, will come into new prominence and enrich contemporary practice.

However, beyond elements of provision there is little that is firm or clarified for teachers to take from the early childhood education tradition. Teachers must fall back on classroom experience and seek to develop professional expertise without much theoretical guidance. Conspicuously absent from the common law of early childhood education is, simply, knowledge about what has actually been going on. The development of a body of knowledge about classroom practice should essentially be conducted against the backcloth provided by the tradition. Each should inform the other and provide a framework for teachers more objectively to evaluate their classroom practices and innovations. On the other hand allegiances to the common law have often lain behind resistance to change. With officialdom supportive of nursery education, this is surely the time to start the task of examining assumptions, techniques and findings of relatively recent classroom-based research in an attempt to build a picture of nursery classroom practice.

David Hartley (1987) claimed that the formal goals of the nursery school tended to be less academic (or instrumental) than affective (or expressive) in emphasis. He commented:

> That is why, in the nursery school, there does not appear to be a formal curriculum which is transmitted by an obviously didactic teaching style. All that one can see, so to say, is the hidden curriculum, for there does not appear to be any teaching going on (p.59).

It seems that the issues outlined by Shipman (1985), concerning the problematic influence of the human sciences on classroom practice throughout the school years, are made even more complicated by the overarching nature of the hidden curriculum in nursery schooling. The role of the teacher, her intentions and behaviour, are features more nebulous here than in later primary schooling. The task of examining nursery classrooms may thus be peculiarly complex and make Shipman's cautionary advice particularly apposite.

In drawing attention to an important characteristic of human beings – their creative capacity to behave with ingenuity and initiative – Shipman warned against determinist laws about human behaviour on the grounds that it was the very ability to behave uncharacteristically that was in question. We should, he advised, direct enquiry towards the context of behaviour, seeking to identify the numerous interconnecting factors rather than trying to develop a handful of lawlike principles, whether of an interior psychological or an external behaviouristic kind.

He pointed out the tendency of researchers to ignore or 'control out' factors that contributed to complexity, including those highly relevant to teachers such as the organization of learning. 'For too long', he warned, 'the focus has been on the predictable, on regularities, on the categories of behaviour, not the capacity of children to do the unexpected' (p.106). And of all the areas where research might be concentrated the most obvious was the most neglected: the classroom itself. And within that arena there was one fact of overwhelming simplicity: the message received was not necessarily the one that was transmitted.

That research is increasingly being shaped to accommodate such concerns can be well illustrated by reference to the project directed by Bennett and his colleagues and published in 1984. In their examination of learning experiences the authors indicated the extent to which the model presented by Walter Doyle of the complexities of classroom life influenced them. They suggested that his model accommodated a richness of interaction between teachers and learners in the classroom environment which previous models excluded, with the consequence that the practical relevance of prescriptions arising from such research was lost.

Similarly, prescriptions deriving from cognitive theory had little practical effect. They suggested, as Shipman also argued, that such theory lacked adequate consideration of the wide spectrum of factors like constraints of time and resources. Drawing from Doyle's model Bennett and his colleagues proposed to investigate 'the crucial features of the environment which link teachers to learners ... the tasks which teachers provide (p.6)' and included as their brief 'the nature and content of classroom tasks and the mediating factors which influence their choice, delivery, performance and diagnosis' (p.9).

Walter Doyle (1986) suggested that the many variables in the teaching context need not be considered in parallel but could be examined simultaneously where they converged. Thus 'academic task' was the concept taken here as an analytical tool and 'subject matter' could be seen in the broad sense as a classroom process. And so 'from this perspective, tasks communicate what the curriculum is to students' (p.366). Task, thus regarded, could illuminate classroom interaction, though care was needed: the same content could be represented by different tasks and of course the task would vary according to the nature of the demand. Children might not accomplish tasks using procedures the teacher intended. Indeed, task was describable at different levels: in the teacher's mind, as announced, as negotiated, and as understood. Doyle accepted that 'it is not unreasonable to wonder where the task **is**' and yet 'this complexity demonstrates the power of the framework to capture significant aspects of what goes on in classrooms' (ibid).

A major insight from Doyle's classroom observations is that 'meaning is seldom at the heart of the academic tasks they work on' (p.374). Bennett et al also found in their study that tasks 'demanding discovery or invention were rarely presented' (1984, p.29). They established that sometimes teachers intended the tasks to include such demands but the actual task demand failed to do so, and sometimes, although the demand was included, the children 'converted' the task. Doyle himself concluded that certain types of task were deemed appropriate for classrooms, fitting the conventions of teacher and children's work systems, and they 'tend to represent the curriculum as discrete skills and procedures rather than occasions for struggling with meaning' (p.377). His implied criticism was clearly that such task types were not only the norm but also of questionable educational value.

Our view owes much to this analysis but it differs from it significantly. It is this: it is the teacher-child interaction that is at the heart of the educational process and it must always be about something. That 'something' is the task, which – if it is routinely conceived as an exercise for skills and competences rather than a problem – will devalue the teacher-child interaction which will become demonstrational, instructional, transmissional rather than the exploration of making sense and figuring out. The more the task becomes problematic – so long as it remains within what Vygotsky called 'the zone of proximal development' (that range within which children can figure it out by pooling ideas or by teacher intervention) – the more effective it becomes as an occasion for teaching and learning. Hartley's view is surely correct:

> The hidden curriculum the teacher constructs and transmits may ironically be hidden from her consciousness ... what is warranted is a more diverse sociological and philosophical analysis of the pre-school, one which complements the rather one-sided psychological perspective which has hitherto prevailed. (p.72).

But Hartley offered an approach, not a tool. In our view the analytical tool for investigating and making sense of the myriad classroom interactions is task, although we concede that that concept is itself far from unproblematic. Some difficulties with the concept have already been outlined but the complexity of the nursery setting provides special mysteries which Doyle appears not to have considered.

Stemming from the child-centredness which contributed to Hartley's plea for a new approach, Tamburrini's (1988) refined definition of an interaction in such an environment gives further pause for thought. She defined three components in an interaction. First the teacher 'needs to diagnose a child's intentions, second to comment on or elaborate them in some way that has cognitive potential, and third to ensure that the child understands her, the teacher's intentions' (p.23). Of course this is prescriptive, and actual research conducted on task reveals that in the classroom environment there are often points of 'failure' in the second and third part. But it is the first part which is of particular relevance here. For in all his considerations Doyle tacitly assumed that direction and intentionality fundamentally belonged to the teacher. Here however, Tamburrini stresses identification of the child's intentions, indicating that direction and intentionality take on a more shared ownership.

Raising serious questions about aims, the point has significance here. It is necessary to add to Doyle's discussion, concerned with where the task is, an extra dimension, relating to the variability of starting point of task within an interaction. And though the origin of the task is fundamentally an issue to do with aims, the nature of the nursery environment is likely to draw this aspect in too, in the course of examining classroom research.

The research to be referred to reflects an emphasis on children under five, though research in infant classrooms is selectively used when it is seen to be particularly relevant. Some of the research investigating the education of the under fives has involved a variety of settings because of the nature of pre-school provision, but the focus here is on quality and factors contributing to it, rather than an interest in making comparisons between forms of provision. The Oxford Pre-School Project, particularly the contributions by Sylva et al (1980) and Wood et al (1980), the study by Hutt et al (1989) and the study by Cashdan and Meadows (1982, 1983) – all conducted in the late seventies (Hutt et al having rather belatedly, though valuably, reported) make significant contributions to the study of 'the classroom'.

The Hutt study, funded by the DES, and each of the others, funded by SSRC, have features in common with the ORACLE project on primary classrooms. Representing a significant move in terms of coming to understand classroom practice they make important observations which yet remain peripheral to our central concern, namely the quality of the pupils' educational experiences. Other research, focusing on particular aspects such as language, play and structure, offer more precise analyses of classroom interactions and valuable insights, without directly addressing this.

In order to use this research to produce a model of the nursery classroom a number of categories have been defined. In reality such distinctions are artificial; for the purposes of analysis however they are essential. It is intended that their definition is firmly founded on considerations of classroom practice. In drawing together aspects of different classroom research studies, and evaluating them in accordance with Shipman's general precepts and Doyle's particular interpretation of classroom interaction, we hope to construct a model of nursery practice that will be readily recognizable to the professional teacher.

It is assumed, as a principle, that in classrooms teachers have the responsibility to teach and children the opportunities to learn. This sounds trite; we wish it were. We feel that much that has come down to us from the traditions of early childhood education has blurred this and other distinctions, which is why we emphasize it now. In order to honour the efforts of pioneers and unsung heroes and heroines we have to disperse the consensual mists. Robin Alexander (1988, p.155) makes the same point, calling for the reappraisal of:

> ...the sanitised, ahistorical, consensual and unproblematic version of primary education as a whole which informal ideology, by a process of hegemony, seems to have generated.

If successful teaching is achieved it occurs within certain structures which we want to break down into two broad categories: classroom structures and tutorial structures. The first includes the shaping of time, space and planned activities, for which we feel teachers must accept responsibility. The second is more dialogical; it is created by both teacher and pupil and is more open to possibility. Following this introduction we shall use them in our evaluation of research studies. First, however, we shall consider those elements of the school which are largely beyond the individual teacher's own control.

'Givens'

Although responsibility for establishing the classroom environment rests with the teacher, she has certain 'givens' to take into account: the features of the working environment for which she cannot individually be held responsible. Coined by Wood et al (1980) in the introduction to their contribution to the Oxford Pre-School Research Project, in which they addressed the role of the adult, 'givens' can include (i) the ratio between adults and children, (ii) the size of the institution and (iii) the physical setting and school philosophy.

(i): The adult-child ratio

A nationally accepted ratio acknowledged by the 1988 Select Committee Report is one adult to thirteen children in the nursery classroom, though in 1986 a national average of 10.7:1 was reported by DES in *Statistical Bulletin 8/87*, with usually less in the playgroup (the two types of setting are administered by different regulations).

In their *Childwatching* study Sylva and her colleagues (1980) observed nineteen pre-school centres in Oxfordshire, consisting of six nursery schools, six nursery classes and seven playgroups, and found a much improved ratio. Margaret Clark (1988) points out that the definition of staff is rather loose in this study since it includes any adult regularly in the unit; this tends to make it difficult to interpret much of the evidence concerning quality of conversation and interactions in play. Students and parent helpers are unlikely to have had much training and the question of adequate training was Clark's particular concern. However, while this caution is of importance in considering some aspects of the research, a sensitive deployment of such adults seems a reasonable course of action and the results are consequently of interest to us.

With ratios of 1:8, 1:9 and 1:10 described as 'good' (p.159) and those of 1:7, 1:6 and 1:5 as 'excellent', the authors noted that activities differed accordingly. Those assessed to be the 'most challenging' were to be found in circumstances where ratios were 'excellent'. They included small-scale construction, art, and work with structured materials. Conversation was judged to flourish betweeen adults and children; children were found to engage in twice as much dialogue with an adult in centres with 'excellent' ratios than in those with 'good' ratios even though, of course, there were certainly not 'twice as many adults around to serve as conversational partners' (p.161).

Alongside Clark's qualification with respect to trained person-
nel lie other concerns about this study including the particular
analysis of 'high challenge' activities and the approach to observation. Nevertheless, that such distinctions could be made between
centres which could all be described as being 'richly endowed with
staff' (p.159) must invite cautious speculation about the effect of
adult-child ratio on the interaction, particularly in the many centres where it is much less favourable. Indeed, Hutt's work (1989)
provides considerable reinforcement.

> The data add further support to the conclusions of earlier chapters
> that a key factor is neither the nature of the materials nor of the
> activities to which the child is exposed but whether or not an adult
> is actively involved in their exploitation ...
> The key to the quality of children's learning experiences is adult
> participation (179). [Hence, Hutt concludes:] Close child-adult in-
> teraction may result in magical changes. What this suggests is that
> a high child-adult ratio is essential if the type of cognitive benefit
> we have indicated may ensue. This points to the need for continu-
> ing commitment to investment in the public sector (p.220).

Regrettably, the Select Committee Report and HMI Report (HMI,
1989) skirt discussion of these important conditions and qualifica-
tions to which Osborn & Milbank (1987) have also drawn attention.

(ii) Size of centre and number of children

The interest Sylva and her colleagues took in teacher-child ratio was
accompanied by a concern with the absolute number of people in a
centre. Centres gave very different impressions, they reported: some
seemed crowded, others intimate. They felt that this must be ac-
counted for by other factors than simply the number of children
on roll. Whilst actual spatial size must have an influence, the wide
variety of uses to which areas were put was an important dimension.
They concluded that no useful classification of spatial size could be
made by them, given the main thrust of their research; instead they
grouped their centres in terms of the enrolment size in order to
consider the effect this had on the activities children pursued.

Although the decision seemed somewhat arbitrary some interesting conclusions were drawn by the researchers. Assuming that cen-

tres with less than twenty-six children were small whilst those with more were called large (p.163) their investigation led them to the conclusion that there was a greater frequency of 'pretend play' in the former, especially amongst the younger children, whereas there was more physical play in the large centres. Smaller centres were also observed to have more engagement at the level Sylva described as 'high challenge'; furthermore there was much greater contact between children and adults. The evidence did not indicate that the large centres were incapable of achieving the atmosphere and engagement the researchers rated as favourable but they had:

> ... a harder row to hoe. They can create an atmosphere of small-ness and steadiness but this feat requires careful planning of pro-gramme and arranging of space ... Neither small nor large centres are home-like. They offer, instead, another kind of intimacy – one easier to achieve with fewer on the roll. (p.165).

This evidence was supported by the research findings of Osborn and Milbank. Children who had attended a variety of pre-school groups were tested at ten years in an attempt to ascertain the effects of pre-schooling in the long term. So many factors overall had to be considered that conclusions of any certainty were hard to draw. Nevertheless one particular finding – that of high test scores achieved by children who had attended home playgroups – was thought worthy of comment, despite its statistical insignificance when considered alongside the results of those who went to LEA nursery schools or hall playgroups. Osborn and Milbank suggested that unless the children from home playgroups over-represented children of above-average ability, despite the statistical controls employed, then home playgroups were singularly effective in promoting children's cognitive development' (p.215).

It was the small size of the home playgroup which was so particularly distinctive, with an average number of children and staff of thirteen and two, respectively, whilst hall playgroups had twenty-three and four, and LEA nursery classes thirty and three. In addition, such groups had the intimacy that Sylva found so facilitiating – probably because they operated in private houses. However, since 81% of home playgroups were located in 'well-to-do or rural areas' (p.216) and certainly received fewer children from referral by a social worker, health visitor or other professional than the hall playgroups, LEA nursery schools or Day Nurseries, they were, it was suggested, least likely to 'accommodate children having any kind of social or behavioural problem' (p.216).

Though this must render any statement about the particular quality of home playgroups tentative, an examination in greater depth might establish that factors including the numbers of children and physical settings, together with an establishment less affected by the demands of bureaucracy than institutions like schools, might help adults to secure more straightforward educative relationships with children.

Hartley (1987) certainly found that the structure of nursery schooling was influenced by bureaucratic demands. Identifying high quality interaction in one sort of setting (for example, the home playgroup) could lead to a reappraisal of constraints in other sorts of settings. In summarizing the studies within pre-school units Clark (1988) added weight to this view in her comment:

> The demands placed on staff working in educational settings with young children may not only be excessive, and ones for which they are not adequately prepared, they may also be in conflict with each other. (p.101-2).

Of course, in contending with these 'givens' the teacher may adopt various stances. But although she is not without power she must act within the parameters laid down for her, the chief and most inexorable of which is the very conveyer belt of chronological age on which she and her children stand and which takes them all deeper and deeper into officially decreed structures. Within this general condition however, and within the constraints imposed by other 'givens' the teacher's decisions are crucially important. In the initial stages of their research Wood et al (1980) conducted a few case studies which made this point very clearly.

(iii) Physical setting and school philosophy

The aim of this research was to examine the impact on the activities and experiences of children that different styles of working produced. The method eventually adopted was to provide practitioners with portable tape-recorders and small powerful microphones and give them the discretion to record as they saw fit. Two teachers, Janet and Rebecca made their first recordings in the early stages which were then categorized to yield the functions the speech was intended to fulfil.

While Janet's tape reflected a high amount of management activities, for example, directing children into activities, negotiating deals, stopping potentially dangerous or threatening situations and attending to wounds, Rebecca's tape was quite different. Some of her time was similarly spent but the emphasis was on play and instruction. This difference, together with Janet's sense of dissatisfaction that her aims had not been conveyed at all through analysis of the transcript, prompted an exploration at this stage into the settings in which the two teachers worked.

Janet was in an open plan school in which each teacher was responsible for particular children. This pastoral duty involved such obligations as seeing the children with their parents when they arrived at school and when they left, monitoring them throughout the session, 'mothering' services, and directing them to group activities such as story time. Each teacher was responsible too for particular 'territory' and events going on within it. Janet explained the idea: 'this system will allow both parents and children to focus on one particular staff member to give security within the open plan' (p.23).

In practice this system, coupled with the high mobility of children in a large area which included a number of rooms and gardens, increased the management demands on Janet's time. In looking at reasons for children to approach Janet the researchers found that it was nearly always for 'managerial help' – access to turns, equipment, fair play or sympathy. When they came to Rebecca however it was usually for interaction – asking her to play, help them to make something ... supply creates demand' (p.25-26). Her school situation was significantly different. She kept the register for a group of children and had particular interest in them but not daily responsibility extending throughout the session. Her immediate concerns focused on space and activities.

Although these complex relationships were considered important, systematic continued study of them was not possible, owing to inadequate resources. However from their observations the research team concluded:

The form that interactions between preschoolers and adults take – what type of activity they are involved in; the time available for chat, play and teaching – is intimately bound up with the physical structure of the school and the fit between the school's philosophy and its architectural form (p.26).

42

We cannot leave the subject of 'givens' without questioning the concept. It may be that it is beyond the capacity of one teacher alone to affect them but the staff as a team has considerable power to effect change. None of these examples is unmodifiable in principle and there is considerable scope for corporate action. Now, however we turn to those classroom structures over which teachers have greater opportunity to exercise professional discretion.

CHAPTER 4

Classroom Structures: Time

In this section we offer a reading of research studies organized to throw light on three crucial classroom structures. Our wider purpose is to encourage teachers to review the classroom arrangements for which they are responsible. Just as schools are structures within wider structures, classrooms are structures within schools and tutorial contexts are structures within classrooms. Structures have unities of sorts, have principles of organization and change, and they share a particularly significant property: they cannot be fully evaluated on their own: they are parts of greater totalities. Here we look at time.

Published in the late eighties Hartley's research project looked at contexts of classroom life for which teachers could and should take direct responsibility. The Scottish nursery units *Nelson* and *Fieldhouse* were matched for enrolment, catchment area and architecture. Another important feature common to both was the declared ethos: 'that the children be given structured freedom, not licence' (p.71). He found similarities in the ways in which nursery school life was conducted. Parents were 'kept at the margin' and children made their choices from the essentially teacher-directed 'sequencing of events' and 'structuring of space'.

Nelson and Fieldhouse were matched in order to identify contributory factors to what differences he found. What really differentiated the two nursery units was the degree of freedom allowed to children. As Hartley summed up: 'The differentiation and specificity of time, space and assessment was greater at Nelson, both for children and, especially, for nursery nurses'. His explanation of the results was that pre-school teaching activities were heavily influenced by two 'tendencies' one of which he named the bureaucratic, stemming from administrative requirements and covering anything from summative assessment to the regularized allocation of time and space for activities. The other he called the idealistic, emanating from child-centred educational theory emphasizing individual choice, self-referenced assessment and flexible time and space allocation.

Hartley commented that while teachers were likely to explain their actions in the idealistic mode, using voluntaristic language, the truth was that much of their actual work was the outcome of bureaucratic requirements. In drawing attention to the strength of the bureaucratic tendencies in schools Hartley echoes criticisms of philosophers such as Peters and Kleinig who both warned against creeping institutionalization. While that is indeed something to guard against, it seems to us that Hartley's was a more neutral point: there always were such tendencies and their effects tended to be underestimated by teachers who, as a rule, exaggerated their own individual responsibility for what they did.

We would differ from Hartley on only two points here: first we favour the word 'agency' rather than 'responsibility'. It is part of our argument that teachers have responsibility whether it is acknowledged or not, that where their actions are unduly influenced by bureaucratic decisions they should consider whether they are justifiable and whether there are procedures for their views to be taken into account. The second point at issue also turns on terminology but like the first it is not simply linguistic. In using the words 'bureaucratic' and 'idealistic' Hartley injects a sharp distinction in value. Indeed in using the vague word 'tendencies' he implies that they are not even the same class of thing. In effect he polarizes the two notions.

But whether they are bureaucratic or idealistic what they have in common is that they are both institutional decisions with educational implications. In making the sharp separation he does, Hartley produces two consequences both, in our view, regrettable. *A priori* it dubs certain types of institutional decisions humdrum while sanctioning others. Now of course at different times some individual decisions will be more important than others. The crucial fact that they have an underlying commonality of belonging to one class of institutional decisions with educational implications makes it illogical to assume that some sorts of decisions are, in advance of and despite any evidence to the contrary, more significant than others.

His general point is, however, well taken. It behoves teachers to be reflectively vigilant about the structures within which they work. Where their classroom decisions are pre-empted by wider institutional arrangements the latter should be reappraised within an educational framework. It may be that the institutional structures in question are for the time being unchangeable – 'given' so to speak – but the chances are that reasons which were once felt to justify decisions may no longer satisfy and change can follow.

To return to Hartley's results, when we recall that the nursery units were chosen in part for their shared aims, the differences in teacher-directed structures between the two might seem surprising. Hartley concluded that the root cause of the difference was that the child-centred aims were implemented at Fieldhouse while at Nelson they remained at the level of rhetoric. But while the latter observation might be true it scarcely works, in our view, as an explanation. Another way of looking at the same facts allows for the conclusion that Nelson was run as a tighter ship according to principles that were different from its officially declared aims. On this reading its practices were not deficient; they were not caused by a disjuncture between aims and practice: it educated in a different way from Fieldhouse.

On the whole we prefer the second reading of this research. There is no self-evidently 'right' way of educating young children, let alone the sort of shorthand phrases that are supposed to identify child-centred philosophy. What there are are numerous ways of setting about the task, each different from the next and all involving countless unique decisions. In writing this book we are well aware that we ourselves are showing preferences and making covert recommendations. But in this country at least we are wary of claiming to be able to demonstrate the superiority of one kind or another. What we address ourselves to, therefore, are important ways in which schools work, seeking to provide a structural analysis which will help the staff of nurseries and schools to diagnosis, evaluate and plan, in whatever style they choose to do their educating.

In keeping with this aim we want now to use Hartley's work as a starting point to discuss the structures we think are particularly significant. The first is Time, which we have sub-divided into the following: (i) Free-Time, (ii) Directed Time, and (iii) Snack Time.

Hartley provided an outline of the sequence of activities in the units he investigated and pointed to much similarity. Both included free time (or 'choosing'), snack time, story time (which might also include sharing 'news' and improvised drama) between arriving and going home. He suggested that the differences already noted between the schools – Nelson appearing more formal and ritualistic than Fieldhouse which emphasized the development of self-control and offered considerable measure of discretion – would be elucidated by examining the procedures and interactions observed within particular 'times'. In particular he provided a detailed comparison of snack time in the two units.

Hutt reported similar sequencing with 'organized periods', usually for story, singing, musical instruments or activities using a disc player, radio or video. In his research there was less mention of snack time. The quantity of such organized periods varied between the four types of nursery studied but in each of them the overall emphasis was on free play.

Although there are undoubtedly exceptions to such a general summary, in addition to those significant differences in detail to which Hartley referred, the picture of relatively uninterrupted periods of time which was conveyed here could be compared with some research suggesting that the experience of four-year-olds in infant schools was distinctly different in respect of temporal sequence.

From her observations in twenty-four infant classes Stevenson (1987) depicted children continually being interrupted by the very teachers who devised the challenges they were working on. The examples were significant: a child purposefully junk modelling had to be persuaded to stop in order to change for PE; a child engaged in complex imaginative play within a social group was required to leave to read to the teacher; children were, as a matter of course, told to abandon play activities in the classroom 'to go out to play'.

She commented: 'Our young children in school need time, unfettered with restrictions, time to see fully through their self-imposed challenges ...' (p.41). Suggesting two reasons for the failure of the infant classes to allow for this she cited first the teacher's primary perceived role as teacher of reading, writing and mathematics, and second the poor teacher-pupil ratio in infant as compared with nursery schools. To these we must at the present time surely add the increasingly general expectation that four-year-olds should conform to the institutionalized routines of the primary school.

From the evidence of these and other studies it has to be concluded that the use of time as a protected context for developing purposeful activities is something which requires some strength of argument and will on the part of class teachers. Not only is it all too easy for teachers themselves to interrupt children's absorbed activity, such may be the expectations of the schools that others – headteachers, secretaries, other children – regularly and routinely do the same, and in doing so contribute to a culture which is almost as subversive of learning as allowing disruptive behaviour to become a tolerated norm.

Our general point is as much ethical as pedagogic. Teachers should, in our view, maintain respect for children. Just as this may entail in certain (and sometimes frequently occurring circumstances) children's admonishment and correction, so too does it lay the obligation on teachers to put the children's interests firmly in the framework of institutional and classroom decisions. If schools are for educating children then teachers should stand up for what are, in their view, the best interests of the children. With this principle very much in mind, we should like to go on to a more detailed examination of the use of time.

(i): Free time

Our discussion at this point concentrates on the essential fluidity of the concept of free time and some of its important effects on teachers. The research by Hutt and his colleagues emphasizes precisely this point. 'Interruptions, which can be shown to be largely adventitious, whether coming from children or other members of staff, often serve to terminate involvement with a particular child' (1989, p.62).

This conclusion is drawn from two direct observational studies undertaken by Hutt in respect of the adult role. They were conducted within the context of a wide-ranging investigation of the pre-school with the intentions of (i) discovering how adults allocate their time among the different roles which the various forms of provision require them to play, and (ii) finding out how they divide their attention in relation to the demands made upon them by the pupils.

For the first of these, adult activities were categorized as 'associative', 'monitorial', and 'non-associative'. The first involved active engagement in the child's play; the second, managerial and regulating activities, and the third such activities as tidying up and marking the register. Variations in the amount of time spent in each category reflected, in large part, the nature of the environment. For instance, day nursery staff dealing with very young children as well as the three- to five-year-olds had more 'care-taking' duties which did not involve children.

Concentrating at this stage on the teacher's time, observations established that on average a little less than 45% of time overall was spent in associative activities, a little less than 20% in monitorial activities, 27% in non-associative time, and just over 10% out of the classroom in which the observation took place. The average span for each of these was 61.2 seconds in associative activity, 43.9 seconds in monitorial activity, and 58.3% seconds in non-associative activity. Meadows and Cashdan (1982) support this with similar evidence. In play children engaged very little with adults, and talk was very limited too.

In view of the observation that activity spans were 'comparatively short', the second study investigated attention spans of adults and found that these were even shorter; adults shifted attention from one child to another and to a 'look/watch' behaviour within the time spent in a particular activity. These are tendencies confirmed by Wood et al (1980). Also, although approached from a distinctly different perspective, Hutt's findings are in accordance with some of the underlying evidence of Sylva's (1980) research into structure. (We should add, perhaps, that owing to their rather different research interests, the implications for structure which Hutt draws are different).

There are problems in the demarcation of activities defined as associative and non-associative. For example, although it is, on educational grounds, perfectly reasonable to prefer associative to non-associative activity, detailed examination might question certain associative activities as inappropriate, whilst certain non-associative activities take a more positive role, for instance, child observations. However, leaving that aside, the research design enabled investigators to pursue the repercussions of teacher actions quite closely. Although Hutt clearly stated 'the quality of the play within the particular activities described is not here in debate' (1989, p.73), he proceeded to make the following three points, interrelated in practice and each illustrating the effects the adult's use of time had on the child's engagement during the free play situation:

• adults are more likely to be found at particular kinds of activities (p.122)
• analysis revealed that girls more frequently than boys opted for activities where an adult was present

Meadows and Cashdan's analysis similarly reported that girls 'were less often far from the teacher' (p.10)

• the activity span of children during free play increased with an adult present, for example, 49.5% increase in 'mean activity spans' in nursery schools, and 27.9% in nursery classes (p.119).

The conclusion is thus of significance:

The effect of the presence of an adult is an interesting one since it may be unintentional. From our data we cannot say children necessarily chose an activity because an adult was there ... This would suggest that the distribution of the adults in the nursery is a key factor in the environment' (p.126).

He reasoned that even within free play situations observed to be 'dismally short', the adult's behaviour, as measured by the time spent at particular activities, together with attention span, was directly influential on children's activity and concentration. Hutt recommended that a flexible, 'transparent' structure be developed, rather than an 'opaque' one (p.230). A crucial feature of transparent structure involved 'both a spatial and temporal rearrangement of duties ... so that two or three adults working with a class or group of children take on clearly different but complementary roles for certain periods of the day' (p.62-3). Hutt and his team concluded that this would allow for some adults to 'interact with children in depth while others adopted a monitorial role to deal with children requiring routine assistance' (p.233).

This is of course a recommendation allowing for wide variations in interpretation and implementation. Given the sharp differences in practice between nursery teams operating in basically similar environments, one would be cautious in expecting beneficial outcomes as a result of following it. Nevertheless, as a foundation for structure to which other features must be added, it is consistent both with an ethical concern and interest in the individual within a social framework and a pedagogic policy of allowing time for thoughtful activities to be sustained.

However some research, notably that of Sylva and her colleagues, focused attention on adult-directed time as a structural feature that complemented free-time. Contrasting with the notion of 'transparent' structuring, it is this more opaque concept which is now addressed.

(ii): Directed time

The passing reference by Hartley to a broad notion of story time and by Hutt to a summary of activities contained within 'organized periods' give but a vague impression, one which lacks information on which to assess the value of particular uses. Hutt distinguished 'organized periods' from 'free play' on the basis of compulsory attendance. Hence adult-planned or structured activities that were optional were construed as part of free play activities. No further elaboration was offered. Sylva developed the notion much further by examining the ideas of 'fixed routine' and 'task-structured programme'. We confess that some of the differences appear to us somewhat fine, not to say slight, and it is therefore not surprising to us that teachers who believed they were following a 'lightly structured programme' which embodied the latter were considered by the researchers to be operating the former.

A 'fixed routine' was taken to refer to a time sequence having three regular activities. These included milk and outdoor play, which children were free to accept or reject. A 'task-structured' programme was one which contained two or more prescribed tasks during the session, of which two were 'educational' in nature and lasted from ten to twenty minutes each. The contrast was thus between strongly structured (fixed routine) and lightly structured (task activity) types of organization.

Sylva and her colleagues comment: 'It should be stressed that centres high on task structure provided a steady diet of free play 'seasoned' with a few mandatory tasks' (p.132). Each of these two types of structure was then compared with a third type – a 'free programme' with 'free temporal structure'. To the team the results were fairly clear cut. About the fixed routine there was scarcely any positive comment. In the main it was found to have little effect. Indeed the older children appeared to engage in more cognitive challenge in the type it was compared with, that is, those operating a 'free temporal structure'.

However, the comparison between the task-structured type of organization and free-structure programme led to the conclusion that the former had 'a positive effect on children's language and intellectual activity' (p.140). When compared with the 'free programme centres' the task-structured programme contained three times as much play with 'structured materials' which, the researchers point out, was an activity 'rich in intellectual challenge' (p.133). Children were found to engage more in this sort of activity out of choice, following the 'mandatory task' period. In addition, the younger children engaged in more interaction and less parallel play, while the older ones had more contact with adults.

Arising from this Sylva and her associates qualified their statements by affirming that it was possible for centres operating a free
structure to achieve similar quality, given that adults were disposed
to engage with the children in shared experiences, but 'we state here
only that a structured programme guarantees it' (p.137). They summarize the implications of their research for structure thus:

> Based on our limited sample, and recall that we observed only
> 19 pre-schools in one county, we believe that the programmes
> most capable of stretching the child's mind are those with a heal-
> thy balance between tight- and loose-goal materials, whose daily
> routine includes a free choice as well as 'enforced' activity, and
> where periods of order are coupled with some of boisterousness
> (p.141).

We have several reservations about this research. We think that,
irespective of their quality, 'enforced' activities set within a daily
routine of free choice will inevitably lead to unfortunate interruptions in the way that Stevenson (1987) illustrated. For although Sylva
and her colleagues differentiated task-structured and fixed routine
programmes in respect of compulsion and the educative nature of
the task, a fixed routine must surely be implicit in a task-structured
programme. This seems to us to follow from the arithmetic since two
to three tasks of 10-20 minutes duration must be slotted into each
session. Furthermore, the quality of these mandatory or compulsory tasks is surely a major factor in both their obligatory and their
educative aspects. This is, we feel, an important point which requires
rather more justification than it received.

The grounds for requiring children to work on these tasks were, as
reported, two-fold. First, as outlined above, children tended to
choose 'high challenge' activities after engaging in the mandatory or
compulsory tasks, so the latter seemed to bring about beneficial
consequences: engaging in such compulsory tasks was 'good' for
children. Second, if there were no obligation then children who were
'anti-adult' or 'withdrawn' might otherwise escape the teacher's
notice (p.137).

We find these grounds unconvincing. One obvious objection is
simply logical: while nobody would argue that participation in a
compulsory task would have no affect on the nature of the child's
subsequent free choice of activity, there are insufficient grounds
for establishing a causal connection between compulsoriness and

subsequent choice of high-challenge activity. For instance in her research related to the play of Sikh children Davenport (1983) demonstrated that home experiences and cultural background make a distinct difference both to the child's exercise of choice and engagement in activities. Again, Dunn and Morgan (1987) found that, along with other background features (with which they inter-acted), sex also had an effect on the free choice of activities and related behaviour. In a different way still, Hutt closely investigated children's choice of activities and picked out such relevant factors as adult style and participation. Given that children's 'free choice' is vulnerable to influences of all sorts, the isolation of prior mandatory tasks as significant in this respect is most doubtful.

The second reason appears to us no stronger than the first. It has both conceptual and practical drawbacks. If there were no obliga-tion (runs the argument) then children who were 'anti-adult' or 'withdrawn' might otherwise escape the teacher's notice (p.137). We are, we confess, rather puzzled by these two descriptors. They seem to beg a number of questions that are exhaustively discussed in the literature on labelling and expectations. 'Withdrawn' and 'anti-adult' seem to cover the non-'normal' range. We would refer the reader to the beginning of this book where the verbal deficit theory was discussed. Can anyone have forgotten that shameful construct of the late sixties and early seventies research: the 'non-verbal child'?

Was Brice-Heath lost in Trackton? And did Labov labour in vain? Are 'anti-adult' and 'withdrawn' children any the less 'constructed' than 'non-verbal' children? To say the least, these are problematic categories. How can any argument featuring such key elements be decisive? And even leaving these worries aside, to what extent can compulsory tasks really benefit the anti-adult and the withdrawn children to whom Sylva and associates refer? The fact that the children were not regimented but 'invited to participate by the attractive layout of the materials' (1980, p.132) is a side-issue: attendance was compulsory. All children were conscripted and exposed to the adult-chosen tasks. Withdrawn children were re-quired to join a social situation; anti-adult children had to conform and stay closer to an adult than they wanted to. To echo Thomas Hobbes: 'Who benefits?'

Under such circumstances, do withdrawn children come out of their shells and anti-adult children become more disposed to co-operate with adults? While the sort of activity selected and the degree of sensitivity exercised by the adult might be effective, these matters were not the subject of this research. And in any event, with compulsion as the basis, the school is most unlikely to assist the development of positive attitudes or help the individual overcome the inhibitions that may be at the root of such behaviours.

Evidence for this conclusion can be drawn from the work of Manning and Herrmann (1988) in their outline of previous investigations by Montagner and by Manning, and current research by Manning and Sluckin. The general conclusion is that the complexity of behaviour in 'problem children' is such that compulsory activities are not only ineffective but counter-productive. As Manning and Sluckin comment:

> Many of the actions of aggressive children relative to the teacher suggest a determination, sometimes explicit, not to be bossed around ... aggressive or disruptive behaviour may follow upon teachers' reprimands or organizing. (p.137).

Here is clear support for our contention that teachers ought to maintain a concern for the individual when considering aspects of classroom structure. The experience of school has to be at least potentially valuable for every child and teachers have the ethical obligation to see, insofar as it lies within their power, that it is so.

When we turn to the educative aspects of the mandatory tasks we find more difficulty. As already mentioned, Sylva and her colleagues categorized centres as operating a task-structured programme where tasks were held to be both educative and compulsory, but the research method focused on detailed observations of the target child. Thus 'educative' tasks initiated by the teacher appear to have been equated with those categories of activities which had, at an earlier stage, been observed to contain high challenge involvement.

There are at least three major problems with this, which we shall outline and then discuss. The first difficulty we have is with the assumptions of this perspective. The initial categorization of activities, with distinctions drawn between high and ordinary level challenge for each activity is, we think, of doubtful validity. Second, the notion of 'educative' or 'worthwhile' (p.132) has a narrowness that would we feel be limiting to a teacher charged with devising structured tasks. Third, it results in a lack of information about the ways in which the tasks were presented and the basis for the teacher's choices.

The initial categorization, based on twenty minutes' detailed observation of the target child, was essentially interpretative and could not have been otherwise. Our concern lies in the extent to which the research depends on the solidity of these categories. For example, when a child was described as 'cruising' or 'watching', what was she doing?   Surely the answer must be: 'sometimes a great deal, sometimes very little'. To build up a true picture a child must, we think, be observed over a longer period and in a qualitatively different way before assertions of any certainty can be made.

Can the following description of activity and ensuing categorization (which was typical of this research) be regarded as adequate? 'Gets up from table with others. All go to next table where S is sitting with cakes, cash register and tray of toy money' (p.39).

This reported activity was defined as a 'three Rs' activity to the exclusion of other activities. But it could also have been described as a 'pretend' activity – another of the categories used in the research. Our point is that both the criteria and the grounds for determining it one way or the other are lacking. Much more than a crudely behaviouristic observation like this is needed before a category can be confidently ascribed. Moreover, when the list of categories is consulted 'three Rs' activities are found to be broadly defined as 'careful, genuine attempts at reading, writing and counting' (p.33). We find it unconvincing that 'three Rs' activities are described as highly challenging, while 'pretend' activities are merely moderately challenging. There is no satisfactory rationale for this. And yet it matters because although Sylva claims that a mixture of levels of challenge is essential, it is the high challenge activity which warrants the adult's attention by providing a compulsory activity.

This does, therefore, seriously limit the adult's vision in planning and presenting a task. Although we have, we think, given reasonable grounds for our doubts about Sylva's arguments for compulsion, we do not wish to contest the obvious. It is beyond dispute that a teacher's undivided attention amid plentiful opportunity for sharing experiences is a fruitful context for the development of valuable dialogue. Our point is that Sylva's initiative was based on the idea that it was the high challenge activities which demanded such contexts. Ours is that learning at this young age may be 'high-challenge' in lots of different areas and the organization of the class ought not to set exclusive patterns, let alone those confined to three Rs.

The sub-dividing of each category into challenging and ordinary levels of engagement – a procedure which depended on judging which categories contained the greater amount of challenging or 'worthwhile' activity – gives rise to a similar concern. Consider the following two extracts describing art activities which the researchers observed and classified.

Art: challenging

Target child (TC) takes paper and a pen, and colours in 'blobs' with apparent random scribbles, but carefully. He takes another colour and fills in a corner. He fills in another corner with a new colour. He takes a stapler and puts staples down one side, and adds a strip of Sellotape. He folds paper in half and staples down the ends. Then he takes a pen and draws round staples.

Art: ordinary

TC is at the table with paper, felt pens, stapler, and Sellotape. TC takes some paper and a pen, and scribbles hard, filling in a large coloured 'blob'. He folds the paper in half and Sellotapes it down, folds it in half again and tapes it, then folds and tapes again (Sylva 1980 p.56).

Sylva clarified 'challenge' in this research as cognitive challenge and while not dismissing 'physical exertion' or 'management of feelings' (p.59) as incapable of high challenge, her distinction effectively separated cognition from physical and affective aspects of the learning process. Add to this the fact that age differences were not taken into account in these definitions of complexity, and examine again the example above. In the example of 'ordinary challenge' the target child has presumably been categorized as more hasty, less attentive, more repetitive, less thoughtful than the target child in the 'challenging' example.

Age and disposition however, if taken into account, could have resulted in the 'ordinary challenge' example achieving the 'challenging' level, whilst the 'challenging' example might be more appropriately viewed as 'ordinary'. Sylva pointed out the lack of distinction as far as age was concerned but did not acknowledge its importance.

The point is that these definitions – not to say (quite) 'standards' – are not in fact capable of the objectivity here accorded to them. They are instead essentially relative to numerous factors. These range from such obvious ones as age and disposition to such constructs as Athey's (1981 p.363) 'persistent concerns' and Tizard's (1984 p.114) 'passages of intellectual search', both of which consider the individual and the active part children play in their own learning.

Sylva's study even provided conflicting evidence. Describing the role of the teacher in task-structured centres she wrote: 'there is actually less adult-led group work but when it does occur it is well-planned and challenging' (p.133). Yet within the same chapter some detail is provided about the children's actual engagement during the compulsory task period which must cast serious doubt on the validity of that statement and the real value of this particular sort of structure:

A not insubstantial proportion of time was devoted to off-task behaviour. Moreover some on-task behaviour was not challenging. Children might wait patiently while instructions were given a second or third time to the slower ones in the group. Or they might be interested in the workmen outside but not allowed to go to the window to watch (p.138).

Though Sestini's research (1987) corroborated Sylva's basic findings about mixed mode structures, she made observations that confirm many of our doubts. Thus her study helps to draw attention to the limitations of any research which observes a target child for 15-20 minutes with the intention of gaining a representative view of the child's activities. Her work also has implications for recognizing 'the functions that seemingly low level activities may serve in children's cognitive and social development' (p.28).

In this section we have considered some of the available quantitative research. Our conclusion is that while much important data has yet to be generated there is at present little evidence to support the view that high quality learning experience in the pre-school depends on adult-directed time as a very specific feature of temporal structure. It is nevertheless an important research theme and we add our encouragement to those who would investigate it. Comparative research in respect of adult-directed time would be particularly relevant, especially if it is as illuminative as Hartley's investigations of snack time at Fieldhouse and Nelson, to which we now turn our attention.

(iii): Snack time

Hartley's description of snack time gives an idea of the value of this sort of research. At Nelson snack time started with children going to the toilet, two at a time, and on return taking a chair each and forming an arc of chairs. A prayer was said together and this was followed by children individually going to the teacher's table to collect a beaker of milk. Empty beakers were returned in similar fashion and exchanged for a biscuit and fruit. In contrast snack time at Fieldhouse omitted the toilet and prayer rituals and was held round a table with an adult. A child served the milk from a tray, during which time the children talked. Typical topics were how many children there were at the table, who were missing, and so on.

It ought to be pointed out that many nursery schools and units do not have a distinct snack or milk time. Where this is the case it often corresponds to the belief that children's time should be interrupted as seldom as possible and that they are well able to help themselves to a drink when they are thirsty and between activities. This view may in turn rest on the assumption that children are more self-regulating than often given credit for and can readily cope with this level of independence. Of those schools and units which do have this 'time' there will be as many minor differences in routine as there are practitioners. The value of Hartley's research lies in his bringing to our notice such particular differences within settings which are otherwise so similar. By doing this he provides the opportunity for evaluation of the rationale underlying the practices.

Our principle remains the same. No particular routine practice is good in itself. It should always be open to reappraisal. In the last analysis each routine is a structural feature. And structural features are themselves parts of a larger totality which could be ordered otherwise.

In this example, snack time at Nelson was characterized by time-wasting, pointless exercises, as illustrated by the toilet ritual. Children of this age may occasionally have to be reminded to visit the toilet but they normally know when they need to go. Their abilities can readily be identified when they are allowed the independence to exercise them. Together with other features of Nelson snack time this practice undermines rather than respects their competence and does nothing positive to develop their self-control which is itself a declared aim of the school.

At the same time it is an inappropriate use of adult time. At the end of a string of instructions and admonitions all that is accomplished is a visit to the toilet and the consumption of drinks and food. For such achievements the ritual was neither a necessary nor a sufficient condition. There is no evidence either that snack time at Nelson was an occasion for sharing, kindness or other genuinely sociable values.

It seems to us, as it seemed to Hartley, that there is little or nothing of educative purpose about such a ritual, unless one counts as educational the reinforcement of the teacher's authority. Snack time at Fieldhouse, on the other hand, contained the potential for co-operation, responsibility and sociability, all rather less ambiguously educational values for pre-school children. If it is not too banal to say so, the purpose and thought we give to situations are likely in part to affect the outcome. In this comparison of snack times Hartley manages to convey the impression that Fieldhouse had reflected on the point of the practice. Research findings, however small-scale, can be particularly useful in steering reflection and contributing to purposeful planning.

In this instance Wood et al (1980) have something useful to add. In one of their case studies they followed a teacher who had been made conscious of her rather excessive use of managerial talk by being presented with a tape recording of herself in action. In attempting to improve her teaching technique she used milk time to make a effort to chat amiably with certain children who had escaped her attention during one particular session. Unfortunately, the researchers concluded, her efforts were frustrated by the very effects her routine practice had produced. They commented: 'the constant demands for management from children persistently disrupt her attempts at extended talk' (p.30).

However, in her investigation into dialogue in the pre-school Robson (1983) found the incidence of 'animated dialogue' at lunch time so high that she advised nursery staff to consider making milk time a small group occasion. Her observations are important to note in trying to offer an explanation for the failure of the adult in the Wood case study to achieve her intentions. She implies that the process is a subtle one, requiring sensitive attention to the setting as well as the style of talk:

Adults who were relaxed and informal and who did not attempt to dominate conversations created the best atmosphere for supporting dialogue. Conversations ranged from the food being served to the day's activities and often children discussed home and family. Complex, abstract language had to be used since events and places were being described from memory (p.145).

This view is analysed from a social and cognitive perspective by Ioanna Dimitracopoulou in her unusual study *Conversational Competence and Social Development* (1990). She combines philosophical analyses by Wittgenstein, Austin and Searle with examinations of empirical studies, such as those by Ervin-Tripp and Gordon. The latter scrutinized videotapes of family conversations for evidence of progression in social competence. They revealed that when other people were talking, two-year-olds simply blurted out requests for 89% of the time, six-year-olds did the same for only 31% of the time and older children used social markers to intervene. Nursery conversations would therefore appear to be extremely important contexts for children to learn and practise the social discourse rules (Dimitracopoulou, p.31).

In paying due attention to the setting in the ways indicated by research there is the increased possibility that teachers will engage in more reflection on the sort of structure they maintain, becoming more aware of the assumptions and influences that affect them and their children's actions and consider, in consequence, the degree of match between the structure and the outcomes they hope to bring about. However time is organized, it interweaves with other structural elements of school and pre-school experience such as space and presentation of activities, to produce the uniqueness of each nursery setting. It is to these elements we now turn, taking first the use of space and second, the presentation of task activities.

CHAPTER 5

Classroom Structures: Space

Hartley's treatment of the spatial structures of the two units Fieldhouse and Nelson is less detailed than his examination of their temporal structures. It is nevertheless a very useful starting point for this discussion for whereas the spatial 'givens' were similar in both places the ways they were interpreted and restructured were plainly different (p.62). In addition, he uses a wider perspective than normal, emphasizing the significance arrangements have in establishing the atmosphere - including teacher attitudes and expectation and sense of community – in which young children operate.

Hartley selects for his research project display space, floor area, and play space (especially the demarcation between indoor and outdoor space). Each example is reminiscent of Doyle's model of the classroom in which, as Bennett et al (1984) describe it, 'teachers and learners adapt to each other and to the classroom environment'.

(i): Display space

Hartley's initial impression was of high contrast between the two nursery units. Fieldhouse's apparently random arrangements resulted in a mass of colour whereas Nelson's organization allowed more of the actual walls and ceiling to be seen, giving the impression of space and order. Mobiles at Fieldhouse were low – just above the children's heads; at Nelson they were closer to the ceilings and were fewer in number. Paintings at Fieldhouse were loosely grouped in themes – jungle, sea and transport, for example. There was no discernible attempt at imposing symmetry, indeed children were encouraged to use stepladders to display their work themselves.

At Nelson the display was in the hands of the staff and symmetry, order and pattern were greatly in evidence. Furthermore, while the prevailing ethic at Fieldhouse forbade the use of templates, the opposite view was taken by the Nelson teachers and their display contained templated shapes in abundance, both two- and three-dimensional:

> One wall was a tiered row of identically-shaped, mass-produced Christmas artefacts: a templated face of Father Christmas, above a mass-produced Christmas cracker, above a Christmas card. The objects were arranged vertically, in sets, one per child (p.63).

When asked, the teacher explained the neatness and balance of the display and the similarity of the things the children made. The clear display patterns made collection by the parents easier and the standardization ensured that no parents could be perturbed by poor achievement by their child: 'all the children do the same otherwise the mothers think their child's neglected' (p.63).

It is worth recalling that in terms of declared ethos the two units were similar, yet here is evidence that the actual priorities the respective teachers observed were markedly different. Although the Nelson slogan was 'the development of freedom through structure' the teacher let that be overridden by what she thought the parents really wanted. While Hartley used the example to illustrate the tension between the bureaucratic tendency and the idealism of child-centred educational philosophy (p.71-2), we are inclined, however, to see it as highlighting problems in overall structure. For us it indicates a need to re-evaluate classroom policy in relation to overall philosophy.

(ii): Floor area

The Hartley, and a small number of other studies provide some evidence that the organization of floor space can have a marked effect on the learning environment. Neill (Dowling, 1988) conducted a small-scale study which implied that adults tend to oversee a range of activities rather than become involved with specific children in large open spaces. This serves as a reminder that in structuring space in the classroom the teacher needs to examine the 'givens' of the location in the light of both her personal aims and relevant public evidence about organization within settings.

Nash (1981) conducted a three year study in Ontario in which children's learning in 19 randomly arranged classrooms was compared with that in 19 classrooms 'in which space was deliberately arranged to promote learning' (p.144). Both types of classroom had the same pieces of equipment and quantities and types of learning materials but in the 'random' classroom the equipment was placed according to 'housekeeping' rather than 'educational' criteria. Thus important considerations were noise, availability of water, reduction of possible mess, dual usage of tables (for lunch), and so on. Sometimes no criteria at all were offered.

The 'spatially planned' classroom was thought out according to learning objectives. So, various kinds of activities were grouped and allotted certain classroom spaces. The general idea was that each group of activities made a contribution to the overall objective of developing the 'child's potential' (p.145) and that each group could itself be analysed into a number of specific objectives. Non-spatial elements were similar in all classes. With regard to time, for example, 75 minutes free play was allowed for after initial registration, followed by a choice of activity on a planning board. And there was an equal distribution of the two kinds of teacher, classified as 'directors' or 'facilitators'.

In the spatially planned classrooms there were four areas, each catering for different kinds of activity associated with the following: (1) number and scientific concept development; (2) oral language; (3) fine motor, visual and auditory readiness; (4) creative skills and ideas. There was, in addition, a fifth with a sketchier remit: 'either indoors or out, with gross motor equipment, motivating props, and ideally, music' (p.145). We find these categories somewhat rough and ready, to say the least, and the language awkward. The distinctions are not as plain to us as they appear to have been to the authors. Nevertheless it is a professionally interesting topic so partly to get ourselves a little clearer, as well as to help the reader, the diagram from the article (p.146) might be helpful.

The Learning Environment

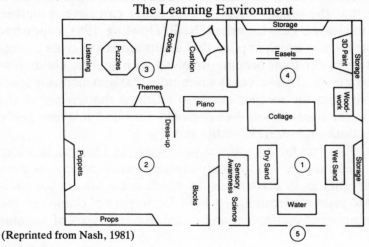

(Reprinted from Nash, 1981)

In order to fulfil the purpose of the research – to see whether the arrangement of equipment according to learning objectives had a measurable effect on the children's learning – each year each child was observed in two or more of these 'learning centres'. The measurements were derived from the specific objectives of the learning programme and agreed to beforehand by the researchers and the teachers.

This is a particularly interesting piece of research, for although it has, in our view, several flaws it delivered a judgment of professional significance: there was a clear difference in the learning outcomes, with children in randomly arranged classrooms demonstrating less evidence of development than children in spatially planned classrooms. Naturally enough, given our general argument that teachers are responsible for the structures of learning which they can change but choose not to change; that they should as a consequence reflect on both arguments and evidence relating to the worth of what they do or allow: given all that, we do of course welcome the Nash finding. There are nevertheless some difficulties and we should like to look at two of them.

First, the measures the researchers used in order to find out how well the children were learning were related, as one would expect, to the spatial planning decisions. For instance, measures in science and number were almost wholly based on Piagetian tests for conservation and measures for oral language used Halliday's instrumental model of language to assess trends towards the use of language for a variety of purposes. Such matching has weaknesses as well as strengths.

The use of Halliday's work in connection with Area 3 is a case in point. When one considers the context of this particular area with its equipment of books, puzzles, a piano, and so on, and the variety of activities that must have been generated, it is obvious that wide ranges of thinking and feeling were stimulated which were not given oral expression at all, so would the Halliday scheme have been the most appropriate measure of what was achieved? Conversely, if the objective was to research the instances of Halliday-type categories they were at least as likely to be found in the other areas. The outdoor and gross motor play area – for which, oddly, there were no measures developed – would surely have been rich in examples.

The second weakness relates to the first for by specifying objectives and measures of learning outcome within each area there is the danger that connections between areas were overlooked. Indeed, account was not taken of the capacity of many materials to promote various aspects of development, nor of the ability of children to adapt materials to their own purposes in unique though characteristic ways, as both Duckworth (1979) and Athey (1981) report and commend.

Looking at what Nash calls (p.145) the rational space plan from this perspective, we think there is more than a suspicion of arbitrariness about it. Why divide the room into these areas? There does not seem to be compelling justification for the arrangement and consequently the larger enterprise is weakened. Ironically, Nash gives as a testament to the virtues of rational planning the words of a four-year-old introducing a new child to the classroom. Described by the author as 'the best summary of the effects of rational space planning in kindergarten', this is certainly that. We have to grant Nash success. This child is a Mozart except that for 'music' read 'pigeonholes':

Over here we make lots of things and here, we find things out. This is where we pretend, and build, and be as grown up as anything. And this is a nice quiet place where the puzzles and books are – you can't ride a trike or play ball or bring sand in here. This is a good place to be.' (p.155).

However, despite these drawbacks the study is very useful. It shows in a casual way how inappropriately some teachers apply criteria to the arrangement of their workrooms. It also demonstrates that the spatial organization can convey to the children something of the teacher's thinking about spatial structure and can, as a consequence, be part of a teaching strategy. In the light of this work the conclusion that children will learn in all classroom environments but not necessarily what teachers intend them to learn, makes sense, as does also its corollary:

Settings planned using criteria other than the advancement of pupil learning often produce distractible behaviour, making it difficult for a child to complete a task without interruption, or unlikely that he will progress to more complex activities' (p.154).

Space planning is a key factor in the structuring of learning contexts. It has important consequences both for desired and undesired outcomes. Our additional point is that such planning should be compatible in aims and values with other classroom policies and with the philosophy of the whole institution. There is a clear indication that the researchers believe that when equipment and materials are close, they are associated in the minds of children. This is indeed part of the rationale for the experiment: that connections are assisted by the planning. For example, in creative activities in spatially structured classrooms children combined materials:

> Frequently using rocks, wood or box-structures, painting them, decorating them with collage materials and threaded beadwork or playdough. (p.148).

while in 'randomly arranged' classrooms, children:

> Painted on paper and rarely combined any materials, except when they painted or pasted box-sculptures or objects made in wood. Such activities were usually set up for one or two days by the teacher, rather than having a number of combinable materials grouped together all year. (p.148).

While we cannot, nor do we want to quarrel with a research judgment that children will adapt materials to their own purposes and that nurseries and schools should make provision for this on educational grounds, we are wary of the rather rigid pre-specified measures adopted: we suspect that these prevented the researchers from taking into proper account even more creative and thoughtful combinations.

To what extent are Nash's spatially structured classrooms compatible with the 'good practice' proposed by Sylva? Referring to one particular centre, Sylva outlined a structure in which, as well as the 'mandatory' tasks discussed above, temporal and spatial structures merged to produce a daily routine in which certain areas were deemed to be 'out-of-bounds' at particular times, for example, no sand play before milk-time. She defended the practice in the following terms: 'If all the activities were available all the time, how can he possibly decide what to do first?'

This seems to us a rather weak justification for a structure that tends to preclude unusual combinations of materials and weaken defences against the development of stereotyped activity. How such strategy is instrumental to the development of children's autonomy and independence, as Sylva claims, is not self-evident, at least, to us.

With regard to 'readiness' activities, the provision of a sheltered space resulted in children spending more time at such activities and experiencing less frustration than children in randomly organized classrooms who complained of interruption and disturbance.

Much of this is endorsed by the High/Scope classroom plan in which 'the classroom is divided into well-defined work areas and the materials in each area are logically organized and clearly labelled, which enables the child to act independently and with as much control over the classroom environment as possible' (Dowling, 1988, p.104).

However, as far as High/Scope is concerned, there is no evidence that this *open-framework cognitive-developmental* model is any more effective than the 'child-centred nursery school approach' with which amongst others it was compared (Weikart 1988, p.29). The Ypsilanti Perry Pre-school project was a longitudinal study. Using the above two curriculum models and a third it reported that the latter – the *programmed learning direct-instruction approach* – was more strongly associated with unfavourable social behaviour than the first two.

We have no intention of even commenting on the fantasy world of tracking down teenagers whose pre-school education was one of three types with a view to judging which type correlated most strongly with later social disorder. But since the Ypsilanti project was invoked, we do point out that Weikart's research does not support the contention that the particular structure found in the High/Scope model is more favourable to learning than the model described as 'child-centred, nursery-school'. The High/Scope research cannot therefore be used to support the evidence collected by Nash. Further, the use of broad categories of structure cannot take account of differences *within* the category. This is particularly true of High/Scope, but possibly also true to some extent of the randomly arranged classroom category adopted by Nash.

The comparison made by Hartley of the two nursery units, Fieldhouse and Nelson, provide an illustration of this. The ethos they shared of 'structured freedom' placed them both within a child-centred, nursery-school approach, yet Fieldhouse, which appeared more randomly organized, with less formalized staff duties than Nelson, had at least four classified activity areas and staff operated a rota whereby a day was spent on each set of activities. Nelson, by comparison, had an art room and a play room, and staff duties were specified in respect of preparation for and tidying up after all the activities.

From the evidence of these studies we think there is a good case for believing that spatial planning should be associated with transparent rather than opaque structure. We explained this notion, deriving from the research by Hutt and colleagues in the 'Free Time' section of the previous chapter and here we simply pick out a relevant point. The main difference between the two notions is that in the opaque structure the teacher and helpers heavily underscore by their behaviour in space and time the relative values of different kinds of activities. As a result the children quickly learn the sort of agenda Nash's child so proudly identified and the diversity, spontaneity and sheer unexpectedness of learning simply ebbs away.

We want to recommend that teachers, with Nash, should look to the criteria they use in placing activities, and consider gathering together particular activities to aid the making of connections or combinations. But they should take care that it is done within a transparent structure so that greater flexibility is possible and children would not conceive of, describe and utilise the different areas of the classroom in rigid terms. We want to maintain that at least two aspects of the study by the Hutts both modify and enrich the work of Nash.

The first of these is that much stereotypical activity in the children's use of materials was observed by Hutt and his colleagues who surmised that the lack of facilities for making connections between materials was a key factor. As they put it:

In our view, staff ingenuity concentrates too much upon particular activities and products rather than upon possible connections between them ... with more imagination and organization the situation could be altered with connections made between activities and events (p.98).

Spatial structuring of activities should be accorded the importance that Nash advocates. However the combinations which Hutt considered necessary to enhance the level of engagement in activities were more extensive and would certainly involve combining activities between 'learning centres' as well as within them. Hutt observed smaller, less rationally structured groupings, called them 'micro-environments' (p.98) and found the maintenance of a distinct identity with little movement of activity between them a major cause of stereotypical and limited use of materials. They give an example of such forbidden combinations that would, if unprohibited, give play greater purpose include the mixing of sand and water to produce sand cakes which might then sensibly be taken to the home corner.

The second aspect of the Hutt study that we want to consider is the concern about that distinct identity, common to 'micro-environments' and 'learning centres'. While Hutt's team thought that both quiet and noisy places should be available within the classroom or nursery they noticed that some activities were associated with certain types of behaviour.

For example, while the collage table was always busy, had an adult in almost permanent attendance, guaranteeing a partner for unrestrained, wide-ranging conversations, the dry sand and water areas were, in contrast, havens of quiet, solitary or parallel play. The quality of play observed in the sand and water areas tended to be repetitive and unimaginative. Adult involvement together with reflection on the purpose and value of all areas of provision should enhance the quality of *all* 'micro-environments' and reduce the incidence of stereotypical play. Again, a transparent rather than opaque form of spatial structuring would enable different areas of learning to be highlighted within a dynamic and proactive classroom structure.

(iii): Indoor/outdoor play space

Curiously, Nash placed comparatively little emphasis on outdoor play. Fundamentally classified as 'gross motor play' the argument was that there should simply be an 'adjacent space indoors or out' with equipment facilitating such activity 'available for the children's use at all times.' (p.145). The published account omitted details of both the activity and the equipment.

This neglect could indicate differences of opinion about the nature and value of outdoor play. Should children be free to use the space whenever they want? Should it be encouraged? Why, what is the justification? Dismissing the ignoble thought that it simply poses difficulties for assessment we think that Nash was probably reflecting a contemporary ambiguous attitude towards the educational value of a taken-for-granted part of the early childhood tradition (See Bilton, 1989). Hutt confirmed from observations and discussions with staff that:

Important quantitative and qualitative differences distinguish play indoors from that occurring outside and that these differences warranted systematic investigation' (p.77).

Accordingly the team conducted a further study of eighteen children in several nursery schools. Equal numbers of boys and girls were observed during the summer months, indoors and outdoors, for equal periods of time. Activities were categorized as material play, physical play, fantasy play, walk/run, look/watch and 'other'. The amount of time spent by each child in the different forms of activities was worked out as a proportion of the total observation period. Physical play predominated outdoors and material play indoors, while fantasy play occupied similar percentages of time indoors and outdoors. The walk/run category was observed more frequently outside than inside, whilst the look/watch category, though more frequently observed indoors, occurred 15.6% of the time outside as well.

In summarizing this evidence Hutt concluded that it reflected differences in the availability of materials and apparatus in the two types of situation. Sometimes outdoor space was observed to contain sand and water trays and easily shiftable equipment such as paint and puzzles, but predominant resources of outdoor areas were the types of apparatus that encouraged physical play. When this was set alongside other findings of the study, for example that adult activity was found to be 'monitorial' more frequently outdoors than indoors, the impression created by Nash finds confirmation.

There was much that this study did not reveal. Fantasy play, for instance, was found to be similarly represented both outdoors and indoors but was not examined for its content or complexity in each situation. Physical play was not subjected to analysis, and it is not even possible to glean from the account whether or not fantasy and physical play combined to result in, say, imaginary journeys to the zoo or the moon or to put out the fire. Nevertheless, by implying that the outdoor space would benefit from the same recommendations made for the smaller 'micro-environment' discussed above, the Hutt study provides some support for developing a purposeful structure both within the outdoor area and between the outdoor and indoor environments. The initial structuring of the nursery environment was considered to be three-fold. Time and space structures have already been discussed; now it is the turn of the third element, the structuring of activities and materials.

CHAPTER 6
Classroom Structures: Task

In our opinion the source of teacher expertise is the ability to diagnose what children should learn next and embed it in an activity attractive to them. The point of the activity has to be clear enough to satisfy pupils that it is worthwhile, should they ask. We sometimes use the expressions 'task activity' or 'classroom task' because those are how Walter Doyle refers to this fundamental and most skill-laden creation of the teacher. The American researcher has impressed us in his various journal papers by the rigour and methodological care with which he has investigated this crucial teaching tool and his ideas underlie much of this section. A task activity embodies a number of decisions, each presupposing knowledge and expertise. It is, in Doyle's own words, 'a situational structure for organizing and directing thought and action' (W. Doyle & K. Carter in Hammersley, 1986). It is a curriculum structure.

One normally thinks of a curriculum as a whole course of knowledge. We approach it as comprising an infinite number of curriculum tasks. But this chapter is about those structures over which teachers can and should exercise control and the fact is that the total curriculum structure and, by extension, the different curriculum objectives are not the prerogatives of teachers, except in heavily circumscribed ways.

It is again an aspect of our total argument that education is itself only a part of a much larger structure of society. Teachers have only limited rights over the selection of knowledge: the broad outlines should, in the case of schools maintained by public bodies at local or national level, be laid down by democratically responsible governments, and in the case of private institutions, by contract between home and school.

But the principle that teachers are not sovereign over curriculum objectives – whether responsible for nursery or school-age children

– does nothing to lessen the importance of the central task. Using their understanding of children they have to select appropriate curricular objectives and devise activities which will embody them. The task activities will, to be successful, catch the interests and engage the minds of children at the right level and must therefore depend on complex abilities of diagnosis and creativity.

The model of the classroom put forward by Doyle and outlined in the first section is especially pertinent here. He pointed out that when researchers set out to study processes such as learning they consciously or not make or assume models. Since under Education Theory One teacher training relied for years on findings from the human sciences, student teachers faced models of learning which posed problems of relevance to their professional work.

They struggled with Piagetian 'schemata' and Vygotskian 'zones of proximal development', justifiably unsure whether these were in some sense real or only opaque metaphors for aspects of the human mind. They received behaviouristic nostrums about clarity of instruction and timing of repetition of such banality that it made them wonder about the spiralling costs of research. Doyle has been a staunch advocate of the principle that if educationally relevant research is required then it should be realistically based. No more speculations about isolated self-developers nor manuals about changing group behaviour.

The arena teachers are interested in is the classroom. The learners who matter are pupils. The conditions must be typical. What is to be learned is the curriculum. In essence, classroom research should be carried out in real classrooms, that is with far from model pupils, in less-than-perfect conditions and with consistent curricular objectives.

What is important is the justification of the structures the teacher thinks are best for classroom learning. And part of those structures is the curriculum. The question is not: should there be a curriculum? There always is. Rather, there are two questions, both inescapably ethical: what should it be and how can I justify teaching it?

Distinct, though related, is the question about the source of teacher expertise: how can teachers devise task activities that will bring together curriculum objectives and pupils in such a way that understanding of something important will be deepened or performance of some ability will be enhanced? It is easy to ask the question but Walter Doyle has charted some of its complexity. He points out, for example, that task activities are intrinsically ambiguous: they are used for different purposes for different children and empirical research (not least his own) has shown that children do not know how to interpret them (Doyle, 1986). Maurice Galton discusses this point with the help of Cowie's 1984 research and provides examples of the learned helplessness of pupils as they feel themselves disempowered by the activities they are set (1989, p.137):

> For example, in a recent observation of creative writing a teacher encouraged the children to draft and redraft stories using the approach recommended by Graves (1983). When the stories were finally completed the children were allowed to use the word processor to produce a final version for inclusion in a book of stories.
>
> Seen from the pupils' eyes, the teacher displayed a remarkable degree of inconsistency. Some children, having produced pages of writing, were made to redraft it further, while others who produced six lines were allowed to use the computer. The teacher was able in each case to justify these decisions in terms of the pupils' special needs.
>
> One child who had written several pages was at a stage where the teacher felt 'she needed to develop her ideas further, they were becoming stereotyped', while the child who wrote six lines 'had concentrated well, which was unusual for him and had also worked well with the other children in his group.' The children, however, were not party to these deliberations. When asked by the observer how they knew when their work was ready to be published, they replied 'we take it to the teacher and he tells us'.

Part of Galton's argument is that young children are far more aware of what is going on than we give them credit for. Time and again the researchers were given accurate judgments by them about classroom events. Why then do teachers not 'come clean' about their intentions and the point of the activities they arrange?

In his 1984 paper Doyle uses 'classroom task' to designate 'the situational structure that organizes and directs thought and action' (p.134). In his 1986 paper it is 'an analytic tool for examining subject matter as a classroom process ... to examine more closely the curriculum *as it is enacted* in classrooms and to consider the issues of instruction, management and curriculum simultaneously in efforts to understand teaching and its effects' (p.365). In the 1984 paper he analyses it into three elements:

i) A goal or product
ii) A set of resources or 'givens' available in the situation
iii) A set of operations that can be applied to the resources to reach the goal or generate the product.

His operational definition is completed by the concepts of 'ambiguity' and 'risk'. Because the context of tasks is evaluative these concepts are important. The first refers to the degree of clarity of the process or processes of achieving the goal and the second to the stringency of the evaluation criteria. The relationship between ambiguity and risk is important. A task may have low ambiguity and high risk – it may be very clear cut with easily measured and standardizable outcomes. Or it may be high ambiguity and low risk, as where children are 'to make something you can take for a walk'. The model admits many different variations, and when we use the concept of task activity or classroom task we assume that it can be given a Doyle-type analysis.

Doyle's is a useful way of approaching an examination of the complexities of the classroom. For teachers to have a sense of purpose and direction they must have intentions. In striving to achieve them they require the children to perform certain tasks in order that they move in the required direction. In this way tasks provide the connection between the intentions of the teacher and the performance of the child. Bennett and his colleagues on the 1984 research study found in fact that the actual task demand presented by the teacher was not always the intended task, which of course denies the possibility of match.

But although task plays a pivotal role in Doyle's model of the classroom, its suitability may still be queried on the grounds that it might not accommodate the potential the child can bring to the situation. While there are references to instruction, management and curriculum in his exposition these concepts are not balanced by any reference to the learner. Similarly his description of 'reciprocal causality in classroom relationships' (1979) implies considerable possibilities for classroom analysis. Yet in his interpretation of it children are seen to influence the situation in terms of modifying task demands in order to make them more explicit and less risky. He does not consider that children might be able to make their own contributions to the construction of suitably open-ended task demands in the first place.

We want to suggest that if tasks are to be truly appropriate and therefore well-matched, they must be responsive to and frequently negotiated with the children. This does not prevent the teachers from having clear aims upon which they can act. Tina Bruce, citing Margaret Donaldson and Gordon Wells in support, puts the point vividly:

'... the quality of early relationships is the key ... At times the adult leads and at times the child. Each takes note of and responds to the other's actions and words (1987, p.136).

We shall return to this point in the next chapter when we consider the study by Bennett and his colleagues on match in the first school.

The research we have already referred to in this section illustrates differing approaches to the structuring of activities, such as:

i) variations within the 'free play' situation in terms of the emphasis placed on different types of material and structuring of materials and activities

ii) variations on the notions of introducing knowledge content into whatever activities are currently being pursued, involving a consideration of topic and theme based work

iii) research which in part provides a response to (i) and (ii) inasmuch as it raises issues of 'match' and presents a case for looking more seriously to the children themselves for guiding the selection of activities and provision of materials. This draws attention to the state of provision within and beyond the classroom in which 'events' of all types – and conversation itself – can become a curriculum focus.

(i) Variations within the 'free play' situation:

For evidence on the different kinds of activity available and the emphasis which should be given to them we turn back to the studies by Sylva and Hutt and add that of Meadows and Cashdan. They confirm the range and its uniformity previously discussed with reference to Van der Eyken (1986).

All three studies provide comprehensive evidence about what goes on in the under-five setting, with Meadows and Cashdan examining nursery school classrooms in particular. Each study was concerned with interaction, so teaching styles and structuring of the environment were therefore considered alongside children's engagement with activities.

Sylva's method was founded in a 'target child' approach in which observations of the children were used to categorize activities. Thus the demands made by the actual provision were inferred from the behaviour of the children's responses to provision. In other words the method in this study was not a direct examination of the ways in which activities and materials were themselves structured.

Meadows and Cashdan confined their research to twenty nursery school classes in Outer London boroughs and were particularly concerned to examine teaching styles, mainly through child observations. Using the 'Child Focused Coding System' they selected children on the basis of teacher rating as either 'well functioning' or 'poorly functioning' (whereas Sylva's selection was random).

They aimed at producing a 'complete written narrative record of the target child's activities and conversations for a brief period (normally three minutes), coded immediately' (1982, p.3). In a later publication they confessed, disarmingly:

> Three minutes is a short time but in practice it was as long as we could manage to keep up an accurate record of either teacher's or child's side of an interaction plus an outline of other participants' behaviour! (1988, p.26).

Children were observed on at least four occasions over two days in each term. The observations were coded according to seven scales:

- Level of activity
- Involvement
- Extent of use
- Complexity
- Social participation with other children
- Social participation with adults
- Distance from teacher.

The authors acknowledge the short length of observation to be far from ideal and it is notable that many overall findings are very similar to the Sylva and the Hutt studies, in each of which children were observed for longer specified periods of time (twenty minutes). Although longer they have, we think, a similar arbitrariness which might have been reduced by observing children working at particular activities or for the full length of one or more sessions.

Nevertheless it is important to note that overall all three studies indicate that the level of cognitive challenge was not high – evidence that cannot be divorced from the other finding that teacher-pupil interaction was also low level. Meadows and Cashdan concluded that children's play was most often goal-directed, thus purposeful, with high involvement. On the other hand, it was low on complexity, being mainly simple, unordered and repetitive, and low too on social participation with adults.

Sylva, however, accepted goal-directed activities as being the ones in which high cognitive challenge was most likely to occur, with engagement tending towards the more 'worthwhile'. Of course, her analysis of activities depends on a specific and rather narrow interpretation of 'goal-directed' but it is significant that while Cashdan and Meadows did not find a direct relationship between goal-directed activities and generally high level engagement, Sylva and her colleagues vigorously pursued such a relationship to the extent of producing recommendations concerning 'balance' of activities and structure of the sessions, a balance in which structured materials were held to be particularly significant.

In an interesting and perceptive article Janet Atkins questioned this view. She wondered if teachers had 'got play upside down' (9/9/1981, p.50) when they attempted to observe its cognitive outcomes. She reminded us that play was often low level and attempting to translate it into goals and purposes was not only fraught with difficulties, it sometimes scarcely made any sense at all. So much, she pointed out, was simply incidental: concepts such as shape, colour, one-to-one correspondence, etc. were only by-products of play. Its real purpose was to stimulate creativity and imagination through the cognitive processes such as observing, conjecturing, experimenting and problem solving. 'Highly artificial, carefully graded and prepared apparatus' was probably less educational than a collection of equipment acquired from 'the local Woolworth's or Tesco's'.

She reported her view that children could sustain play for long periods at home ('when truly absorbed and not distracted') whereas at school they were inclined to flit. Many parents and teachers knew this, she commented, and it was a natural next step to speculate that the structuring of the classroom environment was a top priority if the real benefits of play – 'curiosity and initiative' – were to be won. This, she suggested, required greater adult involvement in play and much less of the 'overtly teaching role'. In spite of this, however, a comparison of children's engagement in particular activities across the three studies reveals interesting similarities. Sand play was, for example, frequently observed to be an activity which children spent long periods at but functioned at a low level whereas art activities which also attracted children for reasonable lengths of time engaged children at a fairly high cognitive level. Moreover, Cashdan and Meadows report, the 'poorly functioning' child tended to engage in the former activity more than in the latter.

Such evidence invites an examination in detail of the way an activity is presented and taken up by the children, but this was not, unfortunately, a feature of these studies. Hartley, however, provided an enticing flavour of this in the comparison he made between Nelson and Fieldhouse which illustrated just how dramatically differently art activities – or even the more specific 'adult-directed art activities' – can be, when perceived, devised and presented by different teachers.

It is salutary to turn to the Hutt research at this stage, for in a similarly comprehensive piece of research a much wider variety of methods was employed. Though broad conclusions were drawn, additional evidence stems from the alternative methods, resulting inevitably in substantially different recommendations. Notably, there was a very detailed questionnaire study in which all nursery staff were asked about their aims and objectives. The responses were closely analysed, and in summary it was reported that the 'emphasis in nursery work remains centred on the child and the need to provide an environment in which he can develop in his own way and at his own pace. This ethos is of great importance in determining the nature of the experiences available to the child in the nursery' (p.57).

The only evidence of real difference was to be found in the replies of the teaching staff. Here there was a clear distinction between those who believed in 'a relatively unstructured nursery environment which has its own unique educational identity' and those who 'viewed the nursery and education available within it as a precursor of the infant school' (p.51). The authors summarize this, observing that the former value free play with limited adult intervention, whereas the latter 'emphasize the development of skills required in the infant school with adult guidance according to a given plan' (p.57).

The teaching role in the nursery is so very complex that this rather polarized distinction is not particularly helpful and in part a product of the particular questions asked. However, there is certainly no uniformity amongst teachers as to their roles and the purpose of provision, as Beardsley (1989) pointed out in connection with differing perceptions of structured play. Many teachers, she suggested, saw it in terms of the materials and objects they set out in a particular area – differing sizes of measuring jugs as part of water play, or medical uniforms and equipment in order to play hospitals in the home corner. That is, just enough to give an indication of the play theme they might follow but not so much as to prescribe and inhibit improvisation.

Others, however, associate structured play with a particular goal or outcome such as learning one-to-one correspondence when setting up tables or trays in a home corner. This is indeed indicative of the distinction drawn by Hutt and his colleagues as a result of the questionnaire they conducted. The connections between such perceptions and actual practice was an important concern for them but it was tenuous and difficult at times to trace. For example, in the chapter concerned with children's use of materials they commented on that part of the questionnaire which sought the views of staff and parents on what they thought the purposes of materials actually were.

Though teachers thought that the provision of materials should generally assist intellectual and language development, the particular purposes behind different activities did not find consensus. For example the purpose behind painting was seen in different ways by staff and parents. Painting was for self-expression and enjoyment, for stimulating imagination, for emotional release. There were even some solid feet-on-the-ground, no-nonsense citizens who saw it as for the learning of colours. While teachers as a group did not represent this whole range neither were they restricted to a single particular purpose. Similar results were obtained for dry sand, water and collage.

As the Hutt team pointed out, activities can have a variety of purposes associated with them and these may vary in relative importance, depending on the perceived needs and stages of the children. Their reference to the literature on children's play is a clear illustration of the varying emphasis that can be placed on the value of using natural materials and the imprecise account of children's needs which accompany this. It is worth quoting the passage in full:

... the accounts of activities may be picturesque products of an adult mind rather than exact descriptions of the child's reality. In particular, the benefits claimed for these activities remain unsubstantiated. Although, as we have seen, sand and water are almost mandatory equipment for any nursery unit, until very recently there seems to have been little endeavour to describe what the children typically do with the materials, or to verify the particular benefits to be derived (p.85).

In the light of this they conducted a study examining what children did with materials provided for them. One activity provided the focus for each observed session, and an individual child would be observed from the moment play with this material began, until the child had finished and moved away. In this way, dry sand, wet sand, water, brush painting, clay and dough, finger painting and collage were scrutinized.

Unfortunately, although there are within the study many useful observations of children there is only limited commentary about the quality of the provision itself. We learn very little of the way activities were set out and managed by the adult. This is ironic as well as unfortunate because in their summary of the research the authors claimed that the quality of the adult management was fundamental to the children's use of materials. In the final analysis the scale of the research precluded an examination of the finer details of interaction within settings and we have to trust that other researchers will fasten upon this interesting topic.

Nevertheless, valuable findings were reported and sharply evaluated. For example, observations of children at play with dry sand revealed repetitive, unimaginative and stereotyped behaviour, with little evidence of interaction with teachers, helpers or other children. 'Why then,' the authors ask (p.97), 'is it so fundamental to nursery practice to provide dry sand for so much of the time? The reason remains obscure.'

Indeed it does. It may be suggested that they studied a collection of nursery schools and classes, day nurseries and play groups in which practice was rather stale, where innovation was rare, but Cashdan and Meadows provide evidence related to sand play which, though scant, is strikingly similar; furthermore their classes were chosen as representative of 'mainstream good practice' (1983, p.2) in the late 1970s. We suspect that future studies will confirm the impression that such findings have general application. The explanations are, as ever, disputable. Hutt recommended for relieving stereotypical or low level play the practice of allowing children greater facility to make their own associations between materials. We have mentioned the bringing together of sand and water already. This may well be relevant. Another possible explanation is the relative neglect by adults of this activity, especially if water is associated with it. We can see no intrinsic reason why such areas should not be rich and stimulating and afford every prospect of fruitful research and experiment. Indeed there is such work in hand.

The research we have been considering serves to illustrate a contradiction that pervades nursery practice, namely that although reports tell us that the provision of materials and activities is much the same across the country and that children and adults participate to roughly the same degree, there yet remain a diversity and lack of clarity about the overall purpose of play and of particular play activities.

It may therefore be helpful to consider the view offered by Duckworth. In an essay in which she considered the relevance of Piaget to teaching children (1979) Duckworth reviewed important Genevan research and used it to put the case that materials should be provided in such a way that whatever level a child was at, he or she 'can come to know parts of the world in a new way' (p.311). Analysing research in which a six year old boy, Didier, was observed working with a set of five Russian dolls Duckworth suggested that even though it was clear he was putting them in order – or to use more technical language, engaged in seriation – no amount of observing could tell the teacher how well, if at all, Didier might now be able to order objects whose size differences were less striking or whose base-line was not already given, as in this instance, by the fact that the dolls stood on the table.

For Duckworth the point was that this did not matter; quite apart from the managerial problems such particular assessment and diagnosis would create, it was fundamentally unnecessary. It might be a problem for Piagetian psychologists obsessed with 'stages' but it was not a problem for teachers. The fact that the activity engaged the interest and effort of the boy allowed the teacher to see what understanding Didier was bringing to the task. She wanted to see what use the boy could make of his present knowledge when faced with a new but related situation. The only diagnosis necessary was 'to observe what the children in fact do during their learning' to gain 'an appreciation of the variety of ideas children have about the situation and the depth to which they pursue ideas' (p.310-311).

Here then is an argument for provision that can be adapted and used flexibly. The teacher may never be certain of the use to which provision will be put, though she will have some idea of the possibilities. Indeed her initial provision of activities is likely to have an essentially arbitrary character. It is true that she may not imagine this to be the case since it will in all probability conform to provision in other nurseries ... But what matters very much more is the teacher's approach, and for this three questions need to be answered:

- In respect of the materials I provide, what do I allow and encourage pupils to do and what sorts of limits do I set?
- In how much observation do I engage and of what type? Is it an open observation of the child in interaction with materials or is my perception framed by my expectations, as it would be if I selected the materials in the first place?
- What do I do about further provision?

This forges a link with the third aspect of this section which considers issues of 'match', but it is necessary first to turn to the second aspect, in which evidence of a rather different sort of provision is examined.

(ii) Topic and thematically-based work:

The studies discussed above considered the presentation and use of rather 'standard' nursery equipment, moreover the research methodology sometimes hindered rather than helped the achievement of insights into promising variations that might have been present in either the provision itself or the teacher's rationale for its use. One of our growing concerns has been the planned introduction of curriculum objectives into the traditionally free play situation of the nursery. This is distinct from, though not a replacement for, the extension of children's experiences within free play.

Typically a topic or theme is introduced. The way in which the theme is selected and presented (at one or at odds with other nursery activities) is undoubtedly open to wide variation. However, we shall consider here only the project conducted by Janet Dye (1984) in the context of the HMI report *The Education of Children Under Five* (1989). Dye's investigation examined the effects of the 'My World' pre-school programme devised by Curtis and Hill in 1975 on the rate of development of normal children. The programme had originally been designed for children described as socially handicapped. As such it had objectives to help children who might have a weak self-image, low levels of concentration and motivation, limited use and understanding of language, poorly developed perceptual and movement skills, poor conceptual and problem-solving abilities and low levels of social skills.

The ideas, activities and strategies of 'My World' were developed into a curriculum intended to meet these needs. Accordingly there were nine themes to be used in sequence beginning with the children themselves and leading towards a greater self-understanding in relation to the wider environment. The themes were: Myself, Clothes, Home, Family, Community, Food, Animals, Transport and Seasons. Fifteen to twenty minutes daily were to be spent on the suggested activities.

She used six schools in North London to conduct the research: three used the 'My World' approach and a random sample of children in these schools formed the experimental group; children in the other schools formed the control group, matched in ability to the experimental group on the basis of pre-test results. Equal numbers of those boys and girls who could understand English – in order that standardized tests could be administered – were used. A comprehensive series of tests was constructed and applied at the start and finish of the five month period of investigation to enable 'pre- and post-treatment performance evaluation' (p.96) to be made.

The findings were clear: the experimental group showed significant gains in the test scores whereas the control group showed a greater level of variability, without at any point making greater gains than the experimental group. There was a significant difference in the overall trend in concentration-span between the two groups. The experimental group improved from the 5-10 minute category to midway between the 10-15 and 15-20 minute categories, representing an average extension of concentration-span of approximately 7.5 minutes. The control group declined slightly from their initial level in the 5-10 minute span. Dye concluded:

The volume, comprehensive nature and quality of the evidence contained in these results constitute a strong case for the existence of a real differential in the rate of development between the two groups. The association between more mature development and the use of the 'My World' programme is established (p.97).

Further testing two years later indicated that the gains made by the 'My World' group were sustained.

A wide variety of checks was used to ensure that the adopted method produced accurate results: in addition to the careful selection of schools that were well matched for staffing, provision and catchment area, visits were made to each class on more than five occasions to conduct 'soft evaluation' in which the sample children were observed with their teachers and nursery nurses in the nursery environment with observations focused widely for comprehensive evaluation of the setting. The project was very thoroughly prepared and is widely cited in support of prepackaged curriculum structures for young children. It seems an appropriate initiative to consider.

The most obvious feature of the original 'My World' programme was the language-deficit model of the child. Since the Curtis and Hill programme appeared in 1975 a number of research studies have clarified our thinking on this subject. Meadows and Cashdan (1988) use the Gordon Wells research (Wells 1986) and the Tizard and Hughes project (1984) to demonstrate that social class related comparisons between 'disadvantaged' children and others relate not so much to language differences but to 'differences in activities related to writing and reading' (Meadows and Cashdan, 1988, p.89).

Gordon Wells and Tizard and Hughes provide grounds for the belief that children are competent, coming to school with a wide range of abilities, but they have differing success in developing and putting to use their abilities; moreover, those children whose background is assessed as working class make up a disproportionately large section of those thus disadvantaged. Further, none of the children observed was more successful at school than at home in demonstrating linguistic or intellectual competence. This led to the conclusion that the practices within the classroom and the approaches adopted by the teachers were in sore need of review.

The information gleaned by Dye from a questionnaire completed by teachers and her soft evaluation in the classroom indicates that the control group had not subjected their practice to overall review, whereas the 'My World' teachers certainly had. This seemed to be a direct result of an in-service course which involved them in practical innovation.

It is arguable that similar results might have been achieved following any course, irrespective of whether the practical innovation involved introducing the 'My World' programme or something quite different. Certainly the observed differences – more innovations, use of more new materials, surprise and responsiveness to children's interests, abilities and aptitudes, wider range of work, greater acknowledgement of the children's own work – are not exclusive to schools operating this programme.

The 'My World' group had fresh adult input each week or fortnight. For example, a display of equipment for bathing a baby or a shoe shop complete with various shoes, boots, sandals and foot measure, all deemed to be 'relevant to children's current needs and interests' (p.99) were included. The control group had, in contrast, less consistent teacher input and less extension of children's interests through the use of teacher resources. They offered a 'good' range of activities but narrower than the 'My World' group. The latter also offered more weekly 'special' activities than the control group, such as shoe-cleaning, doll's clothes washing and face-painting.

As a programme this has the value of being systematic. Moreover, sensitive input of the sort described may well have produced the results Dye found. Nevertheless such input is not, any more than are the approaches described, exclusive to the 'My World' programme. The claim that 'the investigation provided clear evidence that use of the 'My World' programme was associated with substantial developmental gains compared with normal nursery programmes' (p.100) must be qualified with reference to the particular programmes Dye observed in the three control classrooms.

Another drawback to this research lies in Dye's describing this input as 'relevant to the children's current needs and interests' (p.99) whilst simultaneously outlining the total programme as nine themes 'to be used in sequence' (p.96). Holding to such a sequence and claiming to follow young children's interests is organizationally difficult, if not unworkable, and seems to cast doubt on the very processes which produced the findings.

Finally, it must be seriously doubted whether the child-centred principle of following the children's interests is *conceptually* compatible with the insistence on a pre-specified sequence of topics. To claim it to be so seems paradoxical, bringing into question the very coherence of the research concept.

The HMI's *The Education of Children Under Five* (1989) urged teachers 'to combine the areas of learning and experience in a variety of ways' (p.9). The emphasis was on structured activity, seen as part of purposeful play situations, designed to extend and develop children's early knowledge, understanding and skills in ways which provide a sound basis for later education. As the authors put it: 'In the best circumstances, the teaching is informed by a careful assessment of the overall programme and the response of each child to the learning activities'. Thus where – in the view of the report – good practice prevails knowledge content is matched to the child's existing understanding and interest.

Whilst the report outlines general matters of concern its primary focus is on successful teaching, offering 'illustrations of good practice' set within six sections covering the nine areas. Accordingly it is divided into 'personal, human and social learning experiences', 'language and literacy', 'mathematical learning and experience', 'scientific learning and experience', 'technological learning and experience', with 'aesthetic, creative and physical learning and experience' forming an uneasy and cumbersome sixth area. There is much overlap in the examples provided to illustrate each area, and the areas themselves are usefully distinguished one from another (except for the last one which lacks a credible rationale).

Within the general curricular approach the authors give the children their due as active, competent individuals. They stress the importance of pupil choice, and they applaud the exploitation by teachers of both structured and spontaneous events in the classroom and its environs, and the general use of visits.

The report is itself evidence that good practice (as the authors see it) is consistent with many of the implications of the research considered in this section, with the possible exception of Sylva et al. (Indeed 'structured materials' are referred to relatively little, taking their place alongside a wide variety of other activities considered to be contributive to children's cognitive development.)

Its major defect is its failure to clarify the process by which curriculum themes originate. For example, in the section, relating to Personal, Human and Social experience the authors observe:

> The work people do provides many valuable starting-points for learning about the interdependence of human communities and the contribution of individuals to the common good. Given appropriate resources, doctors, nurses, postmen and fireman are some of the roles which children often choose to adopt in their play (p.13).

An example follows of imaginative hospital play in which detailed provision, conversation and structured play fostered 'high quality' engagement which, it was claimed, provoked different types of thinking and feeling. However the work was prompted not by a child's initiative or a child's recent experience of being in hospital or hospital visiting but by staff involvement in an in-service course on the National Writing Project. How much more significant it would surely have been if it really exemplified what Joan Tamburrini called 'the teacher's extending role'? (1981, p.140).

Similarly, work on holes and tunnels in another nursery class followed a very interesting and carefully planned development but its foundation seemed not to lie in children's manifested interests. It did not spring from the observations that children were making holes and tunnels in the clay or sand, poking holes in the soil, climbing through and between large apparatus and expressing fascination at being hidden from view. Rather the work featured as one of several 'carefully selected themes based on the immediate environment and embracing wide human and social experience' (p.14).

In contrast, a third example described a more broadly titled theme 'Around and About' and outlined work which stemmed from walking in the locality and taking photographs of buildings as well as of children standing at their own front doors. Not only was the work which resulted highly innovative, its starting point was much more genuinely collaborative between teacher and children. It cast a wider net more deeply. It offered more possibilities for each child to find his or her own individual focus of interest within the theme than were to be found in either of the previous examples.

Although the examples illustrate the richness of the experience a good nursery classroom can offer, in order that children really can benefit from this richness and make it 'their own' it must have an appropriateness for them that is more evident in the third than in the first two examples. Despite its wide framework the HMI document similarly mistrusts the idea of self-initiated learning. In our opinion the report does not differ so significantly from the Dye research in terms of its message. It is with the intention of pursuing this idea further that we now turn to the third aspect of this section.

(iii) Match:

This section starts by looking at work carried out by Sestini (1987). It directly questioned assumptions underlying both the Sylva and Hutt research and has implications for the quality of learning and classroom practice. Further research provides support and indicates ways of improving the accuracy of matching task activities to children. Children have to put up with work situations in school which often place them under considerable pressure. How do they cope with the demands, both cognitive and social? Sestini observed a random sample of four-year-olds in twenty reception classes and ten nursery classes. She established that the targeted four-year-olds were able to 'adjust to markedly different learning environments and expectations within each setting' (p.26). However, the settings all presented some problems and the study serves to caution us that children's apparent ability to adjust socially and emotionally to a new setting is not in itself an indication that they have made what might be termed a 'pedagogical' adjustment.

In each class Sestini made fiften-minute observations of four children, noting activities, aspects of social behaviour, cognitive demands of activities, use of language, and role of adults, using Sylva's (1980) criteria of characteristics of children's play for evaluating the challenge of activity.

The children in the nursery classes tended to select and initiate their own activities, while those in the reception classes were directed by the teacher, with 'free play' following periods of directed work. The play was quite closely rule-governed and children did not elicit teachers' involvement. Most of the teacher-directed activities conformed to Sylva's definition of 'high yield', containing tasks with structure and goal direction with children working deliberately with concentration. Just a few activities were 'occupational' and 'low level'. Sestini commented about the reception class activities:

Frequently, though the activity was cognitively complex, there was evidence that some target children were not being challenged by the tasks and examples of novel, creative and imaginative activity were rare. Only occasionally, target children showed evidence of difficulty in meeting the basic demands of the task set though there were wide differences in what children were able to produce. A few children had difficulty understanding the instructions given by teachers (p.27).

It seems that so-called 'high challenge' activities neither necessarily matched and stimulated the learner, nor regularly provided experiences which develop the creativity, imagination, reflective and critical thinking at which teachers aim. In the nursery classes observed by Sestini the structured activities similarly met the high challenge criteria. But in this setting there were more adults and they tended to become more involved than colleagues in reception classes. They also had fewer structured activities to monitor.

Nursery class children engaged in high level activities when adults were there, which tended to be with structured activities, but the bulk of their time was judged to involve comparatively low level engagement. Of course, occasionally, peer play achieved a high level of involvement and challenge. When this occurred however, Sestini reported, there seemed to be three factors in evidence. There was usually specific provision by teachers, the activities were strongly characterized by imaginative social role playing, and the children were highly aware of the interested presence of adults in the background.

Sestini's general conclusion was that when there was little or no adult involvement play tended to be low level and repetitive, primarily serving social functions. However she qualified this by commenting that periods of observation lasting no longer than twenty minutes limited the study. Although it was quite sufficient in the case of high level activity to allow her to draw her conclusions, in the case of low level engagement it could be too short for a pattern of learning to emerge. This is an important qualification, on which we have commented in our review of other studies, for it draws attention to the observer's ability to perceive the patterns of children's learning activities and foreshadows possible invalidity in the results.

Again, the general point is reinforced: there is no substitute for extended, genuine, serious and close observation of children, whether researching or teaching. Sestini provides a description of the teacher's role with which we completely agree: 'Interaction is a crucial element. The teacher's role is demanding – provider of stimulating materials, observer, alert to children's interests and using knowledge of how best to develop social and intellectual competencies in children who are at different levels and who have individual needs.' (p.30).

Sestini's study provides a basis for reflection on the issues involved in this. It is clearly important to consider activities described as high level as problematic; high level structured tasks need not in fact provide high challenge to the individual child, as Bennett, Desforges and others confirmed in their 1984 research. In contrast, low level activities may be tackled by children thoughtfully and systematically, with a wealth of personal experience.

Sestini refers to Chris Athey (1981) whose research indicated that children may be 'fitting' while they are 'flitting' (p.363). Athey focused on child behaviour in a research-project nursery here at the Froebel Educational Institute. In this, activities, outside visits and parent participation played an important 'real' part in supporting rich and thoughtful nursery provision. Her contention was that children frequently followed paths of interest that would be unseen by casual observers but which a skilled nursery teacher could recognize and deepen. This, though, should not be accepted as an explanation which reduces the teacher's responsibility to examine provision and its use in respect of the contention that much appears to be low level.

Athey's view was based on observations made of twenty pre-school children during the course of their two-year attendance with their parents at the project-nursery. The project aimed to find commonalities and continuities in their behaviour. In all 5,333 observations were analysed. Each observation was subdivided into seventeen variables, including, predictably, details of the children and the materials. One of the less standard variables was, for example, levels of exploration in which motor level, symbolic representation and thought level behaviours were recorded. Thus the interest lay in the form of behaviour underlying specific content. Athey concluded that explorations were *systematic* for she identified what she called 'schemas of action' underlying a wide range of apparently different instances of children's activities, unifying them as examples of the child's 'persistent concern'. As she put it:

They are fitting various kinds of content into a particular schema. All the project children without exception, showed sequences of behaviour which had schematic bases and the parents became increasingly skilled at reporting interesting instances. (p.363).

She argued that the nursery curriculum could be planned along more educative lines if teachers were to shift from arbitrary content-centred provision ('tomorrow we will do frogs') to provision based on 'recognition of children's persistent concerns' (p.366). And fundamental to such a shift was the involvement of parents in a complementary partnership.

It was this that Tizard and Hughes found lacking in their 1984 investigation of 30 four-year-old girls. The research sample (originally both girls and boys, see Walford, 1990, p.22) were selected to provide two groups, representing working class or middle class families, and all the girls attended one or other of nine nursery classes within the state sector in the mornings, and were at home with their mothers in the afternoons. The children were observed at home on four occasions for two and a half hours and at school for an equivalent time. The researchers were impressed with the quality of the children's talk at home in which they were engaged in 'passages of intellectual search' (p.114). They were behaving as persistent and logical thinkers, actively struggling through their conversations to understand. But in school:

> The questioning, puzzling child was gone: in her place was a child who, when talking to staff seemed subdued, and whose conversations with adults were mainly restricted to answering questions rather than asking them, or taking part in minimal exchanges about the whereabouts of other children and play materials (p.9).

Tizard and Hughes suggested, as indicated above, that one reason for this was a lack of genuine parental involvement in schooling. For while the mothers of the children shared with them experiences which formed a common background for intellectual searching, and the facility whereby that searching could be resumed in various guises, the teachers knew very little about the children's lives outside the school and the use of shared experiences as a classroom teaching rationale was as a result very limited.

Moreover, provision in school might not stimulate that intellectual search to the same degree that the daily routine experiences at home and in the locality appeared to. And clinchingly, the teachers' managerial style of talk foreclosed authentic conversation by its focus on play activities rather than events outside the school context. Just as with Athey's research, the implication here was that, to make really adequate provision, the individual child must be closely observed, listened to and taken seriously. Accurate diagnosis could not be done quickly nor on skimpy evidence. Parental involvement could at one and the same time enhance the quality of education and enable a more complete understanding of the child to be gained by the teacher.

Both Athey and Tizard and Hughes indicate a development of provision beyond the existing play and topic variety, and the latter suggest that this should take place in a re-organised classroom context in which staff could provide many more opportunities for wide-ranging conversations. This is fully supported by Wells (1984, 1986), Hughes and Westgate (1988), Brice-Heath (1982, 1985) and Robson (1983) in respect of language development and classroom conversation, and Mercer and Edwards (1986, 1988, 1989, 1990) and Jackson (1987) in respect of negotiated classroom control in the interests of children bringing their existing understanding to bear on the classroom environment.

Research, then, can help to provide a framework in which both re-appraisal of classroom management, and a deeper understanding of what children do in the classroom and ways in which they learn in general, can lead to provision of activities which would both challenge the intellect and engage the interests of children who are motivated to find ways of understanding the context of their lives. In the nursery setting such a framework should ease some of the problems teachers have in forming accurate diagnoses and following them with suitably extending, challenging input. Bennett and his colleagues identified such problems in their 1984 study and with Joy Kell he produced further evidence in their research into the experiences of four-year-olds in infant classes (1989).

Nevertheless, in the final analysis, what constitutes suitably challenging provision can only in part be guided by research. There remains an essential element of interpretation which must be guided by the educator's beliefs about purpose and intention.

In the course of this chapter a clear theme has emerged. We have tried to look at early education from the point of view of parents and children as well as teachers. When parents send their children to school, what do they hope for? We think they hope that they are entrusting their children to people who will take that trust seriously and regard the children as people in their own right, with their own cultural backgrounds, their own temperaments and personalities, and their own understanding of what is going on. Our view is that teacher-expertise consists of observation, diagnosis, reflection, treatment and evaluation. With this in mind we turn to the structures which for us lie at the heart of education – the particular tutorial contexts in which pupils and teachers come together.

SECTION THREE: A STRUCTURAL APPROACH

CHAPTER 7

Tutorials

Introduction

The Quality of Pupil Learning Experiences was published in 1984. The study by Bennett and his colleagues of teachers and children at the infant-junior divide in primary schools is justly celebrated as a well-designed small-scale but effective research project into how well teachers diagnose pupils' learning and provide learning experiences for them. It is in our view a fascinating book which neatly divides commentators into two groups. There are those, such as Maurice Galton and Marten Shipman, who view it against the background of the ORACLE research project into primary schools in the mid-lands, and draw implications for the organisation and management of learning for older children, and there are others, such as James Willig and Joan Tamburrini, who set it in the less formal and more individualistic tradition of education of the younger child.

In their 1988 essay 'The Experienced Curriculum' Bennett and his colleagues reflect on their study. They write (Clarkson, p.107):

> What this study has revealed is that a number of cognitive aspects of this environment appear to have been hidden from teachers. These have been carefully specified, and their possible consequences outlined, not to carp or criticize, but as a basis for improvement. Teachers will, we hope, accept them in this spirit, for their information, reflection, maybe even inspiration. For improving the quality of pupil learning experiences is as much their aim as ours.

Maurice Galton (1989), having spent much of the previous decade with the ORACLE research, publishing its final volume in 1986, felt the Bennett findings confirmed that teaching ought to be more systematic, managerially, pedagogically and in terms of curriculum objectives. Given our interest in the tutorial we wanted to see how he would react to the notion of 'the clinical interview' – a sort of tutorial for diagnosing and evaluating children' thinking. For Galton it is unrealistic:

> Attempts to diagnose pupils' learning problems using the suggested 'clinical interview' technique would be extremely difficult . . . Without the use of some independent learning strategies in combination with 'direct instruction', the model must – like that of 'Plowden progressiveness' – remain an impossible theory.

Shipman (1985) as part of the general sweep of his argument saw Bennett and his colleagues as having affinities with the taxonomist Bloom because they blamed the teachers, rather than the children, for the poor quality of the work. The twin problems were, he said, misdiagnosis of ability and bad classroom task design, but they were both compounded by a somewhat perverse classroom teaching style which combined group seating with individual working. Although the teachers of these six- and seven-year-olds were selected as high quality the results of their provision were so worrying as to point to the need for remedial inservice. Not only did the individual instruction style cause management problems, it was virtually inevitable that teachers would have to pitch the work at the middle level of ability, with the result that numbers of children would be mismatched. The more competent ones would be reduced to consolidating exercises while the less competent struggled to understand the tasks.

As befits the author of a book on the management of learning Shipman discussed general managerial rules within the classroom. He welcomed the new basis of research in empirical classroom observation and warned that the individualistic child-centred view which seemed so pervasive in first school posed, for those who held it, particular problems. Although he kept his counsel about the degree of formality he preferred, he thought evidence showed confusion and contradiction. As he lightly but memorably remarked: 'The descriptive evidence suggests that teachers tend to adopt methods that minimize the chances of being able to maximise learning.'

The other view on the Bennett research may be represented by James Willig (1990) who welcomed such close attention to match. He is in no doubt that it is expertise in match that is generally lacking

94

and recommends that teachers give the highest priority to developing it. He quotes as illustration of his interest the 'Fiona' passage from Bennett's book (Bennett, 1984, p.175):

TEACHER: Well you ought to be able to oughtn't you. And your pencil's thick and black for a start. That's squashed together. You've forgotten how to do this? You'd better practise at home this weekend. How many twos in five?
FIONA: Two.
TEACHER: Where does the two go?
FIONA: In there.
TEACHER: Write it down on the top. How many left over?
FIONA: One.
TEACHER: Now what do we say? How many twos in . . .'
FIONA: Four.
TEACHER: In what? How many twos in . . .?
FIONA: One.
TEACHER: No.
FIONA: Five.
TEACHER: How many twos in . . .?
FIONA: Four.
TEACHER: But that isn't four. What number is that?

[Shades of Brice-Heath – see later]

FIONA: One.
TEACHER: But you can't say how many twos in one, can you? Because there aren't any, and that's your number. How many twos in . . .?
FIONA: Fourteen.
TEACHER: Yes now come on. You were busy talking and you're stopping other people from working as well. You're getting a bad habit of talking Fiona. You're doing far too much. Right come on. Do this one: 51-3

Of this Willig wrote (p.14):

You can easily see that it is the mechanics of the exercise that pre-occupies the teacher. Over and over again she asks, 'How many twos in . . .? However, there was no attempt to discover Fiona's understanding of the problem or how, if left to herself, she would go about solving it. Apparently it was the rules of 'carrying' that confused her and it was this aspect that needed to be worked on.

His interest is diagnosis and the Bennett research impressed him:

> This book is one of the most important studies of primary schools in action published in recent years, and it is well worth reading for its down-to-earth advice on the everyday problems confronting teachers (p.14).

Not content with earmarking this aspect of the research he went further to argue that in teaching, diagnosis was merely a starting point. Once the problem in a pupil's thinking was diagnosed, an appropriate classroom task-activity could be devised. He names one of his research students, Greg Lancaster-Smith, as someone who undertook this as an aspect of his personal research and recorded the results in his dissertation. There is a particularly telling sequence in which the researcher investigates why a nine-year-old continually fails to work out the correct answer to a subtraction sum. The researcher established that the child had no problems with subtraction *per se*. It was the formal written procedure he could not manage. Lancaster-Smith took the child back to an earlier stage of concrete manipulation of objects and devised a task-activity involving Dienes apparatus which would allow both him and the child to focus on the transition from 'natural' subtraction to formally coded subtraction. The diagnosis was used to work out a more expertly matched task activity.

This is a theme of Willig's book: diagnosis in itself is of little use. It must lead to the preparation of appropriate activities. Willig's approach is very different from the one we looked at before. Diagnosis, individual attention and personalized teaching are what teaching rests on. Of course, it is not easy, but in a real sense, if they are lacking then so is teaching. It is a perspective from learner-centred education, or the early childhood education movement.

The approach is also to be found in the paper 'New Directions in Nursery Education' (1988) by Joan Tamburrini, Willig's former colleague at the Froebel Institute. Early childhood education is a highly specialized and expert field in which intellectual development for children and high levels of professional expertise for teachers are as important as in any other educational age-phase. Informality must be understood as a complex structure in which children's development is met through 'educational dialogues' within a thoroughly understood but informal curriculum.

We find the Teacher-Fiona sequence considerably more disturbing than do Willig or the researchers. How can this be a high quality teacher? The Brice-Heath dialogue we shall quote in the next section from her Trackton USA research is genuinely funny because the child is the satirist, the outsider, mimicking the teacher. But this is, if at all, only superficially comic. Isn't there inside this lunatic vocal structure a trapped child who can see no way of escape? It is commonplace but nevertheless deplorable. Why does it happen so frequently?

Geva Blenkin (1988) draws, like Tamburrini, on work by Margaret Donaldson, particularly the notion of 'embeddedness' (see Ch.7 of *Children's Minds*). Blenkin claims that a major task for the teacher is to help children to develop the ability to move from 'embedded' to 'disembedded' thinking: children start school with much cognitive experience that is directly relevant to the nursery and classroom. When the classroom tasks 'embed' calculative thinking children can often solve problems which will quite disconcert them if presented in an 'unembedded' algorithmic way. In the Bennett example no-one could suppose that Fiona could not manage the division if it were embedded.

Blenkin considers ways for teachers to help children to accomplish the necessary but difficult general transition to more formal modes of thought through re-presentation. Conversation has a particularly important place in the curriculum because through conversation – or the more formal 'discussion' – the teacher can encourage children to re-present events, people, situations, to imagine them differently and to view them under different aspects. Although it is not difficult to see in this advice allusions to computer models of mind which appear at an ever-increasing rate in the cognitive development literature, the general argument that such manipulation of images and experiences plays an important role in decentring children's thinking, freeing it from the here and now, is well-made. Geva Blenkin recommends the work of Copple, Sigel and Saunders and his colleagues as very relevant to the task of helping children to develop the powers for formal thinking.

Alongside this emphasis on re-presentation Blenkin draws attention to the 'metacognitive' aspects of disembedded thinking. The central idea here is that such a mode of thought requires an awareness of the tools for thought – ranging from reading to the classifications of objects. The awareness of such tools, the ability to use them, the appropriateness of their use, and so on are part and parcel of formal thinking. Insofar as it is directed towards the ability to handle disembedded thinking therefore, the teaching of young children requires that they be brought progressively to reflect on how they should tackle this or that problem, what materials they need, what plans they should develop.

It does perhaps go without saying that – at least where educating young children is concerned – the diagnosis of mistakes and misunderstood concepts in children's thinking needs time, patience and dialogue, and the devising of appropriate activities needs knowledge of the children. Considering the Bennett research from this perspective gives a different picture.

Yet is it so different in outcome? The danger of closely defining a position is that one puts up fences. It then becomes tempting to iron away internally at inconsistencies. Those 'out there' are simply misguided. In Willig's book there is a certain, probably deliberate looseness. It is a perspective not a theory. It has a point of view. The author obviously values the disciplines of knowledge and methods of enquiry. He has sections on 'telling' and 'instructing' and planning pupils' experiences. And yet he insists that following and developing children's interests are as integral to good teaching today as they were 150 years ago to Froebel, after whom his and (our) college was named. He would dispute those two words 'and yet'. In his own words:

> Whatever policy is adopted, whether it is subject-based, a topic approach, some form of integration or child-initiated learning, the subject-matter of the academic disciplines must directly or indirectly be integral to much of what is learnt in schools. I would also suggest that the form of organization schools adopt may well be secondary to observing such principles as fostering children's curiosity, taking heed of and following up children's interests wherever we can, learning by discovery and the emphasis on first-hand experience that are central to child-centred education and that inform the chapters that follow.

We should not leave this section without paying some direct attention to the Bennett study, although there is probably little that has not been said about it already. Its findings were the following, in summary:

1. Many less able children were set tasks which were too demanding
2. Many more able children were set tasks which did not demand enough of their intelligence
3. Many of the tasks were not appropriate to bring about the learning intended by the teacher
4. As the year progressed the less able children had increasing demands made on them when consolidating tasks would have been better
5. Correspondingly the more able children, after initially receiving a few higher order tasks received an increasing amount of practice items
6. Teachers spent virtually no time listening to individual children's strategies in carrying out work (they did not give children the opportunities to articulate their thinking)
7. When talking to individuals and groups they asked questions almost entirely of a low order nature where factual recall was sufficient answer
8. Teachers tended to teach, not diagnose – the apparent answer to a child's problem and misconception was to re-teach rather than provide a new tailor-made learning experience
9. Teachers often used a double-queueing system at their desks which allowed no time or opportunity to do more than tick or cross work – what Bennett called 'make do and mend'
10. Although children were often arranged in groups they rarely engaged in collaborative group-work. Their arrangement was mainly for management not pedagogic purposes
11. When teachers were tutored on how and when to diagnose, and then returned to the classroom, they found it difficult to sustain any attempts at diagnosis and instead reverted to teaching very soon after
12. Teachers were largely unaware of the ways of dealing with cognitive problems of match and mismatch
13. Children did not take on enough responsibility (or were not given it) for their own learning
14. Teachers were not skilled at asking questions of the type that would provide an insight into a child's misconceptions.

Findings never really stand the passage of time and by now these look, when examined individually, fairly unsurprising. Also, for findings from empirical research, some have a distinctly *a priori* look, numbers 1 and 2, for instance. Others are simply *déjà vu*. Is not number 10 reminiscent of ORACLE and does not number 14 recall Ted Wragg's *Classroom Teaching Skills*? Are not numbers 9 and 10 familiar from HMI Reports and is not number 11 an inservice chestnut which goes way back? It is not the findings which merit commendations such as Willig's.

We do have some quibbles too. We are unhappy with the confident use of 'able' and 'less able'. The terms are shorthand descriptors, inferences from evidence of some sort; how reliable are they? Children we know of six and seven are not easy to categorize. Is an 'able' child someone who has performed certain tasks in arithmetic or is 'ableness' used generally, as say 'smart' is? It is because we find it difficult to draw such conclusions about young children that we feel uneasy. Then again, we feel that the classroom tasks on which the team based its evaluations were somewhat narrow. Arithmetical manipulation and writing seem to be chosen more for their algorithms and measurability than their depth of significance. The team claims Doyle as a kind of doyen behind its thinking but Doyle insists that classroom tasks should be meaning-related; it is the grappling with meaning that matters. What the match was being measured by seems trivial. If children of this age are trying to make sense of things pretty well all the time, it seems to diminish a concept like cognitive conflict with its challenge to states of understanding, involving shifts of understanding, to represent it by variations on sums.

Finally, the theory of learning used by the team is very information-based. Norman's work is geared to the processing of information, whether called knowledge or data. It fits measurement scales in the classroom and helps the team to obtain results, but one has only to compare it with a theory of judgment such as that of E.A. Peel to see that it is much less well adapted to the development of *understanding* where there may be no linear progression but rather a succession of interpretations, than to the acquisition of information and knowledge.

Thus, rightly or wrongly, we have our reservations. They do not prevent us from applauding the success of the study in highlighting the importance of the tutorial context. In our view – and we have reiterated the point throughout the book – the tutorial, however casually entered into, however informal, is where the teacher learns to listen and watch and be open to what the child brings to the situation. The tutorial can be used for the exchange of confidences, to try ideas out, to sort out puzzlement and to diagnose strengths and weaknesses. The singular merit of the study is its graphic illustration of how one can move from product to process – from the 'answer' a child gets, to the way he or she arrived at it. And from there to devising a matching activity.

To paraphrase Kant: matching tasks cannot be provided without diagnosis, and diagnosis is pointless without matching tasks. The procedure of following diagnosis with the provision of matching tasks operates in a spiral fashion, inasmuch as it is part of a continuous process rather than a periodic assessment. Such a notion is linked to the process of reciprocal interaction in setting tasks. In such a process there must be regular dialogue with discussion and negotiation. Within this, diagnosis will have a vital though not an exclusive part.

In the study by Bennett et al diagnosis was shown to be a central problem. Recognized as crucial in analysing 'cognitive confusions prior to the provision of adequate explanations' (p.217), it was found that basically teachers did not diagnose. They were observed to react to the product of the task performance by re-teaching in order to correct the error. But diagnosis requires examination of the child's moves. It clearly demands greater interaction between the teacher and the pupil.

Theories offering explanations of how children learn can help. Duckworth (1979) for instance, whose work is unfortunately dismissed by Bennett et al as being impractical, does in fact, make some very useful comments on diagnosis. From her conclusions that the child makes use of whatever knowledge she already has, when in a new situation, she claims:

> The only diagnosis necessary is to observe what the children in fact do, during their learning. This is not a diagnosis of notions; it is an appreciation of the variety of ideas children have about their situation and the depth to which they pursue their ideas (p.310-11).

In terms of the concern of Bennett et al for specific diagnosis, and relating this to three- to five-year-olds, it is of interest to note the work of another of our colleagues Chris Athey. Discussed by Bruce (1987) Athey's research has been used by certain education authorities, notably Sheffield and Cleveland, to help nursery staff in the process of analysing the actions of young children. Athey, as we remarked in Chapter 6, recommends teachers to look beyond the activities children are engaging in to try to identify their persistent concerns. Her work is intriguing because it also offers another perspective for the examination of classroom-based research. It sheds, for example, an alternative light on claims in the Oxford Pre-School Research Project that 'high-yield' activities in comparison with 'unstructured informal activities... do not challenge the child's elaborative capacities' (Bruner, 1980, p.60). It also emphasizes how 'open' a good teacher ought to be in terms of observing and listening skills, which brings us neatly to our section on creating the conditions for tutorial contexts.

The teacher-child dialogue

The longitudinal Bristol study 'Language at Home and at School' directed by Gordon Wells (1984, 1986), 'Questioning at Home and at School' by Brice-Heath (1983) and Tizard and Hughes' 'Talking and Thinking at Home and at School' (1984) illustrated that from a very young age children display a much wider linguistic competence at home than at school. (Presumably this is not true of adolescents who would normally lack the frameworks to speak academically at home.) This difference in children's behaviour misled some teachers of young children into making inadequate provision for classroom language development. Wells looked at children starting school at five, while Tizard and Hughes focused on four-year-olds who attended nursery classes. Thus, certain of their observations differ: Wells refers more to teacher direction whereas Tizard and Hughes emphasize problematic aspects of free play. Nevertheless, as Wells concludes: Tizard and Hughes 'corroborate the Bristol findings, almost point for point.' (1986, p.87).

The most significant finding is that the reduced level of linguistic competence is directly related to the role teachers play in dialogue. It was found that not only did teachers dominate talk but they did it in particular ways: they made many more requests, asked a higher proportion of questions and initiated more conversations than did parents, all of which resulted in a more passive role for children as they found themselves 'trying to answer the teacher's many questions and carrying out his or her requests' (p.87). Indeed Brice-Heath actually found in her research in 'Trackton' USA children mimicking what they called teacher questions. She quotes Lem who, after his first nineteen days in nursery school, was travelling home by car:

What color dat truck?
What dat truck?
What color dat truck?
What color dat coat?
What color dat car?
What color . . .

My response was: "What do you mean, What color is that truck? You know what color that truck is. What's the matter with you?" Lem broke into laughter on the back seat, realizing his game had been discovered. During the first weeks of school he had internalized the kinds of questions which occurred in teacher-talk centred tasks, and he was playing 'teaches' with me. In the next few weeks, Lem's game in the car was to ask me the same kinds of questions he had been asked that day in school: 'What color dat?' 'Dat a square?' 'What's dat?'.
(Brice-Heath in Hammersley, 1986, p.122)

This wickedly accurate sending up, which Martin Hammersley selected for his casebook of research, was complemented by Mehan's 'What Time is it Denise?: Asking Known Information Questions in Classroom Discourse' in which children are faced by disconcerting responses to their answers, for example:

'What time is it Denise?';
'2.30';
'Very good, Denise' (Hammersley, 1988, p.85).

Again, the general point is that the schoolroom is a teacher's world which needs interpretation by children and self-reform by teachers.

Both Wells and Tizard and Hughes categorically denied that schools provided an environment that fostered language development when compared with homes, concluding that for no child, regardless of home background, was the language experience of the classroom richer than that of the home. Each study attributed this finding in part to the staff-child ratio and in part to the teachers' approach. Wells, referring to the child-centred slogan 'start from where the child is', argued:

What better way of knowing where they are than by *listening* to what they have to say; by attending, in the tasks that they engage in, to the meanings that they make? (p.101).

Tizard and Hughes recommended a change of priorities for teachers, in order to:

> Harness the interest and curiosity which children show at home . . . instead of the present emphasis on fostering play, on devising ingenious ways of using play materials, and on questioning children about their play, a higher priority would have to be given to widening the children's horizons, extending their general knowledge, and listening to them talk. We found that most of the intellectually challenging conversations at home took place at times of relative leisure for both mother and child . . . they rarely happened while the child was busy with an activity' (p.261).

Interesting corroboration by Williams (1986), within an admittedly small-scale study of eleven adults from three schools, affirmed that children initiated very few sequences and that usually adults were more concerned to follow up their own topic of conversation. She concluded that this indicated the little progress made over the past few years in 'putting the interactionist view of the acquisition of language into practice in our schools' and recommended that 'it is essential that the adults working with young children re-assess their role' (p.81).

The research by Wells and Tizard and Hughes, supported by Brice-Heath and Williams, corroborates the evidence presented by Wood et al (1980), Sylva et al (1980), Meadows and Cashdan (1982 and 1988) and Hutt et al (1989). Wood established that much dialogue in nursery classrooms is managerial. Meadows and Cashdan found nursery schools to be busy, happy places but commented that sustained conversation with an adult – along with high complexity of activities and creative, exciting discovery as being 'conspicuously rare' (p.13). They suggested three main reasons:

i) The demands made by the situation on the staff. They commented: 'looked at from the teacher's end we saw an incessant, even frenetic stream of comment, provision and caring; but it was rare for three consecutive 'bits' to be addressed to the same child . . .' (pp.13-14)

ii) The ideology of 'a simplistic, non-interventionist free-play curriculum'. Here they observed that in situations where adults saw themselves as fostering intellectual and social growth subtly and indirectly by providing a 'stimulating environment' and not through their own direct support 'the children see them as benevolent providers of goodies – not as interesting people to discuss things with' (p.14)

iii) the question of aims. They considered many nursery school teachers to be 'traditionalists on the defensive' who implied that their critics were suffering from an 'intellectual version of the Protestant Ethic' (p.15).

Meadows and Cashdan declared themselves unmoved by such a charge; not only were intellectual excitement and rigour and creativity desirable in themselves but 'happy absorbedness' and 'intellectual challenge' need not be incompatible in the nursery school.

Sylva found that when it did occur conversation between adult and child frequently took the form of a tutorial chat. Though this sort of dialogue was not always adult-initiated it served the purposes of encouraging the child towards elaboration of the task involved and diagnosing what he/she understood of the task, rather than conversation *per se*. She commented: 'Most tutorial chats are situations in which the child knows that the adult knows that the child knows the answer' (p.90). Examples of these situations in the study illustrate the measure of control the adult exercises in dominating the dialogue in just the way that Wells and Tizard and Hughes confirmed.

Arising from the Oxford Pre-School Research Project Wood and Wood (1988) pursued a study concerned with questioning the pre-school child, on the grounds that the available research claimed that most talk between adult and child seemed to be characterized by much questioning by the adult. This was a small-scale study in which one teacher worked with three pairs of children, each taking part in at least five stylistically different ten-minute sessions. The authors were concerned that some questions – though not most – were demanding and that teachers who engaged most in questioning were least likely to (i) be asked questions back by the children, (ii) receive answers and elaborations of answers in response to questions and (iii) encourage children's spontaneous comments or contributions overall.

They found that it was not just questions that elicited high-level responses from children which were the problem. The study found that though high-level questions resulted in high-level responses 64% of the time, stringing questions together resulted in low-level replies. It also confirmed that children responded to teachers' speculations and reasons with high-level replies 55% of the time. Wood and Wood argued, accordingly, that if further research confirmed this then teachers might:

> Have their conversational cake and eat it too. For it would follow that they are able to stimulate children to think and reason in discourse without paying the price in terms of children's relatively low initiative and loquacity which a lot of questions entail (1988, p.180).

The projects to be examined in the next sub-section specifically address the role of conversation in language development, in particular the reciprocal nature of genuine dialogue and the degree of control the child has in initiating and pursuing conversation. The teacher's task is seen less as the 'provider' of language and more as the conversational partner who listens and responds, extending and questioning children's speculations, who advances views and is subject to correction. It is in this way that the adult provides what Bruner has called 'scaffolding' to support the child's learning.

It appears from many paralinguistic or pre-linguistic studies with babies that children behave in such a way as to elicit such behaviour from the adult carer. Bower, for instance, considers that infants need such cooperative adults to foster language development (1981, p.112); Bruner (1983) even calls the adult a 'language acquisition support system', while Snow's (1979) study of two babies and their mothers over a period of fifteen months confirmed that mothers behaved as though the 'conversations' they had with their pre-speech babies were intentional and meaningful for both participants and this has been developed in the work of Trewarthen and Huby at Edinburgh.

Although parents may vary in how much effort they put into their involvement, they assume their roles naturally and continue them way beyond infancy, as Wells amongst others has confirmed. When children enter institutions catering for their education and care that function diminishes as the new adults are influenced by organizational and pedagogic matters. Children too adapt, as separate studies in 1987 by Jackson and Schostak demonstrate, and conversational engagement as the medium of intellectual search is easily lost, as Tizard and Hughes found.

But although children may rapidly adjust to the hidden curriculum of schooling we should not conclude that their drive 'to make sense' is necessarily abandoned: the children's vulnerability and the adult's responsibility are highlighted by the research of Hughes and Grieve (1988) which examined children's responses to bizarre questions. They established that children attempted to answer questions even when they were unanswerable as they stood, finding that while seven year olds qualified their responses, indicating uncertainty, five-year-olds supplied additional context to the situation and replied with certainty.

The authors commented that the young child was constantly perplexed by a lack of knowledge and tackled problems 'by making something of whatever information is presented to him . . . most, if not all of the time' (p.151). The young child, that is to say, tended not to question the assumptions but demonstrated a capacity to concentrate on striving to provide solutions, whether or not they were to be found. Thus a heavy burden of responsibility lay with the teacher to develop an awareness of the child's perspective and operate accordingly.

Classroom studies

Three studies which reappraise the teacher's role from this perspective are Dolley and Wheldall (1987), Robson (1983) and Hughes and Westgate (1988) and we shall consider these in turn.

1. Dolley and Wheldall: Teacher Style

This study called upon a nursery class teacher to make use of 'incidental teaching procedures' (teaching strategies developed from the work of Hart and Risley) in order that she might learn to adapt her style to encourage child-initiated conversations. It contrasts with earlier language-learning programmes that were highly structured and adult-dominated, resulting in a 'shutting out' of children's initiatives.

At the Centre for Child Study at Birmingham University five observation sessions over two weeks monitored the transactions in order to provide a baseline. After this the teacher was introduced to the incidental teaching procedures and seven observations were taken in the subsequent three weeks. Finally, four children who had seldom taken conversational initiatives were targeted over five sessions during a further two week period. During each session twenty-five minutes of the teacher's linguistic behaviour were sampled, using a transmitter microphone, whilst observers watched through a one-way mirror.

The results showed that although there was a high degree of variability between sessions there was a significant (20%) increase in the teacher's responses to children's initiatives, while the targeted children prompted interactions five times more frequently towards the end of the project than at baseline. Although the results have to be interpreted with care – particularly the influence of the Hawthorne Effect – this study of conversational style usefully isolates for the teacher one crucial factor and shows that new techniques aimed at consistently following up child initiatives can be learnt and applied. As the authors comment, the teacher signalled:

Her availability as a willing conversationalist, by her readiness not only to contribute, but also to listen, and perhaps most importantly of all, she learned to wait for the moment the child would choose to initiate. When this occurred, on almost all occasions, she was able to elicit elaborated language from the child' (p.289).

The final two studies to be considered take a broader perspective of the classroom yet draw complementary conclusions.

2. Robson: Child-Child Dialogue

Using unobtrusive radio microphones Robson 'listened in' to children's talk in the nursery. Target children were recorded in the 'natural' settings of nursery classes, schools, one nursery, and one special nursery class attached to a school for pupils with language difficulties. Two children were targeted in the latter and ten from the other settings. Of these ten, five were considered to have communication problems while the other five had no such difficulties. The children were also watched, so that important contextual information, which could help to explicate what was going on, could be gathered.

From the recordings it was noted that older children help younger, less mature children and those with communication problems by providing a model for imitation that eases the path of both integration in the group and the acquisition of new linguistic concepts. Many instances were also recorded of 'direct teaching' in which the older children noted errors quickly and could often understand very indistinct speech. One child, for instance, helped a younger child who had difficulty with the consonant blend 'th' to say 'panther' instead of 'pamfer'. Sometimes errors brought ridicule but usually this was when the error was an uncharacteristic slip; children were tolerant of those with speech difficulties and listened patiently without making negative comments.

Robson thought that this sort of help occurred within contexts that were especially conducive to practice and experiment. Such contexts were, she contended, by far the most important factor in language development. The focus of the study made it possible to pick out areas and activities of the nursery which were rich in dialogue and where teachers could teach indirectly by facilitating children's exchanges where the direct intervention of the teacher would have been counter-productive.

In fantasy play and role taking some of the most complex language was produced. Sometimes adult presence inhibited dialogue, however it was also noted that a particular style of adult involvement encouraged the flow of complex language, the example being given of a nursery nurse who took the part of a child while Jane, a child, took the part of her mother who invited her to play with the snow. The exchange is worth quoting for it provides an example of what Hughes and Westgate referred to as a relaxation of the traditional teacher-role (1988, p.15), illustrating the control this allows the child to assume. 'C' stands for child and 'N' stands for Nursery Nurse (183, p.144):

C: Do you want to make a snowman?
N: Yes, aren't you going to help me make a snowman?
C: And don't you get all wet.
N: No, all right.
C: I expect you need your mac on.
N: Oh, all right.
C: You've got to 'ave your mac on.
N: Do I have to put my mac on top of my coat or do I have to take my coat off now?
C: You'll have to take your coat off. Now put your mac on.
N: Right. Excuse me!
C: What?
N: My buttons.
C: I can't keep coming out 'ere. There you are.
N: Thank you.

By contrast, outside activities were not conducive to dialogue of any sort, the recordings revealing a paucity of constructive conversation. Robson suggests that more monitoring of children's time spent outside and greater structuring of activities is necessary.

In general, Robson noted that parallel play, which involves no interaction or cooperation, featured much of the time, also that activities such as sand and water play, painting, modelling and puzzles were particularly conducive to parallel play. This corroborates the studies conducted by the Hutts. Robson provides an example of associative play indicating that 'cooperation on a task is much more likely to produce interesting dialogue between children' (p.145). Accordingly, she suggests that teachers might so structure activities as to encourage more children to participate cooperatively.

She confirmed too that while child-child dialogue followed a similar pattern to conversation between adults with a series of comments and statements with occasional questions, the style of dialogue between child and adult in the nursery was markedly different, with interaction frequently initiated by the adult, in the form of a question often requiring yes/no responses. 'If staff made more comments and statements to children, the latter would have wider scope in response since there would be no right/wrong judgments. But patience is extremely important. All too often adults initiated interactions but did not wait long enough for the child to respond before moving on to the next child or supplying the response themelves' (p.147).

Of particular interest was the evidence that many children used language which was more complex than that used by the adults; recordings provide examples of peer dialogue that used intricate linguistic structures involving abstraction and reasoning. Robson, as Wells and Tizard and Hughes also suggested, argued that staff should be aware of the degrees of linguistic competence children might have and that dialogue with them could be at a higher level of complexity. Since she also suggests that children with language problems benefit from dialogue with peers as well as specialist adult individual attention, the onus must be on the adult to develop a flexibility of response to match the competence of the child.

3. Hughes & Westgate: Positive Structures

The third study serves to draw together the consistent evidence gathered by research to provide a structure within which teachers and pupils can communicate naturally about things which matter to them both.

Hughes & Westgate addressed the issue of what communicative options are available to pupils, with a view to offering structures which would fulfil a wide range of purposes. Four groups of children were observed, ranging from three- to four-and-a-half years of age, the first two in nursery, the second two in reception classes. In order to analyse the dialogue a concept described as 'participant structure' was used. This labelled a typical arrangement of speakers and listeners linked in a communication network, for example, a teacher speaking to one pupil whilst assuming that others were listening. It was assumed that the possible dialogical variations would be related to the variations in participant structure. These structures, argued the authors, 'seemed to present a variable over which teachers might be able to exercise some judgment and control' (1988, p.9). Six participant structures were identified:

1. teacher talking to the whole class
2. teacher talking to a small group
3. teacher talking to an individual, with or without auditors
4. one child talking to the whole class
5. children talking in groups, without the teacher
6. child talking to child, one to one, without teacher.

Each structure was examined and examples were provided to consider the opportunities pupils had for exercising and extending their competence. In (1) pupil-initiative was almost eliminated, with pupils required to attend to what was in the teacher's mind. The researchers suggest that within this structure teacher-intentions are easily translated into patterns of dialogue which put children into roles both limited and limiting. Similar results were found in structure (2) situations, even when the group was as small as two.

In (3) there was a tendency for the teachers to withdraw the 'pedagogic agenda' and allow talk without any preconceived teacher-intention. When this happened pupils relaxed and took time to make their meaning clear, while the teachers both encouraged and sharpened the children's expression. It is worth recalling the observation by Sylva that classroom conversation often took the form of the 'tutorial chat', in which the teacher was concerned to further the task in hand rather than engage in more open ended dialogue.

Hughes and Westgate caution that such dialogue tended to be confined to structure (3), if it occurred at all.

There were variations in structure (4), depending on how the teacher shaped the context, but even when children were relaxed enough to take the initiative the teacher was still responsible for turn-taking and deciding when one pupil had spoken enough; the option of genuine dialogue was thus still foreclosed.

Thus, although each of these structures produced variations, the commonality was, as the authors put it: 'When the teacher was present a form of talk predominated in which the pupils had little scope to do other than respond briefly and within a narrowly confined dialogue structure dominated by the teacher's status and pedagogic intentions' (pp.14-15). Participant structures (5) and (6), in contrast, contained language forms and strategies markedly different both in quantity and quality. Children initiated, extended and concluded topics, and competed openly for turns, and the dialogue was characterized by pupils seeking and gaining assistance from each other.

Hughes and Westgate found, as did Robson in her study, that such dialogue 'revealed aspects of their communicative competence which remain hidden in those participant structures created by, and implicitly also valued by the teachers' (p.13). Further, children talking one-to-one seemed even more able to explore and develop a topic than in a group in which interruptions and overlap are more inevitable. In this participant structure children were observed to collaborate and use skills to solve a problem or develop an idea.

Hughes and Westgate's research indicates that there is considerable dialogical diversity in the classsroom. They go on, however, to argue that in view of the importance recent researchers, such as Mercer and Edwards, have attached to collaboration between adult and children in negotiating meanings certain structures ought to be emphasized at the expense of others. In particular, they maintain, the 'pedagogic agenda' should be relaxed in order to allow more prominence to genuine adult-child dialogue where 'teachers stimulate, take seriously and even challenge pupils' expression of their own ideas' (p.15). They conclude: 'The greater professional control, based on awareness of complexity and consequences, may provide both the justification and the confidence enabling teachers of young children to entertain such change' (ibid).

Whilst the study does not report on time currently allocated to each type of structure and therefore does not distinguish between classes, particularly nursery and reception classes which might well be markedly different, it is exceptionally valuable in providing teachers with a way of reflecting on their own classroom environment, and progressing from observation and identification to action and implementation. But it is important that the notion of relaxing the pedagogic agenda is not misunderstood as being similar to a laissez-faire approach. It is essential to think here in terms of teacher intentions that are flexible and responsive to children's initiatives.

Tutorials

The studies looked at so far in this chapter establish for us certain parameters for the tutorial. Wells, Tizard and Hughes, Brice-Heath and Mehan all produce evidence that teacher-pupil dialogue in the nursery is characteristically different from that in which children engage with their parents. Furthermore, the researchers find little justification for the school forms of dialogue. There are many more research studies than those which we have considered but ours are typical. Looked at from the children's angle dialogue with teachers is all too often a pretty strange affair. Our three chosen studies all addressed this phenomenon. Dolley and Wheldall showed that it is possible for teachers to be helped to reflect on those patterns of interaction which to them seemed natural but to pupils coming new to the classroom, artificial and strange, and having reflected, to make significant changes. The Birmingham University project emphasized precisely this: allowing for pupil initiative in dialogue with teachers.

Robson's research complemented that idea by enquiring into classroom dialogues in which the teacher played no part. While she reported that the quality of dialogue bore a strong relationship to the area of nursery activity in which it took place (which seems well worth following up) Robson's major point was that children were able to, and did, engage cooperatively in helpful dialogue which to judge by its outcomes had to be described as educationally successful. She thought that teachers could learn from their styles of interaction and modify the ways they engaged in conversation with children. Lastly, Hughes and Westgate diagnosed a particular problem which was, in their view, interfering with dialogue between teacher and child, namely what they called with vicious alliteration 'the pedagogic agenda'. They recommended relaxing that agenda and offering up the initiative far more to pupils.

Since we have maintained throughout this book that we think the tutorial context is potentially the single most important structure in school it is clearly important for us that it functions properly at the basic level of communication. The three studies we have just summarized seem to us to help in this regard by indicating how easy and 'natural' it is for professional teachers to establish a climate which could foreclose options and initiatives from children. In closing this chapter it is perhaps worthwhile to cast a little more light onto that shadowy pedagogic agenda which Hughes and Westgate discussed. In the words of Vivian Paley (Paley, 1986, p.122):

> Soon after leading these discussions, I became a kindergarten teacher. In my haste to supply the children with my own bits and pieces of neatly labeled reality, the appearance of a correct answer gave me the surest feeling that I was teaching. Curriculum guides replaced the lists of questions, but I still wanted most of all to keep things moving with a minimum of distraction. It did not occur to me that the distractions might be the sounds of children thinking.

Something similar was said on this side of the Atlantic when the proceedings of Parliament were first broadcast. It is not that the interruption of pre-laid plans is to be sought or welcomed as somehow signifying that educational or democratic processes are going on but it could serve to remind us of the point of the gathering in the first place. Certainly, we would suggest, when the 'gathering' is as purposeful as a tutorial it is imperative that the pupil should think aloud and benefit from the careful evaluation by the tutor.

CHAPTER 8
General Principles

The past is not a series of mistakes that has yielded a modern en-
lightenment. All ages make their best and sincerest accommoda-
tion to their circumstances. A sense of the evolution of classrooms
and schools goes with a sense that their future is in human hands,
though not in the hands of any individual or group. A feeling for
the presence of the past in the present may help us to contribute,
with due humility, to the making of the future (Golby, 1988).

Here at the Froebel Early Childhood Collection Archive in the
Roehampton Institute where we are writing this we cannot disagree
with Michael Golby. Throughout the last few weeks we have been
conscious of three centres of thought: the bookish tradition which
surrounds us; contemporary research which at last is showing us
children and teachers and families and schools as we know them to
be, and the company of professional teachers thinking seriously
about their practice. All three are part of the discussion which we
have tried to reflect.

It is by now fairly clear that we think that educating young children
is a highly expert activity. Teachers need knowledge of curriculum
theory, they need diagnostic powers, they must be self-critical, they
must be alive to the structures they work in and create, and they have
to be critically informed about developmental theory. They should
know that they work out of a powerful tradition and they should be
politically literate. There are no doubt other desirable qualities but
those are some which have emerged as we have worked through
these chapters.

We should like to say one or two things about each of these
centres, beginning with the tradition. It is easy to be seduced by
powerful writing into supposing that nursery teachers are the in-
heritors of a relatively seamless cloak of knowledge which won't

114

stand up to scrutiny. Thus Ronald King in his various writings, for example, *Informality, Ideology and Infant's Schooling* (1988) repeats the litany of 'developmentalism', 'individualism', 'play as learning' and 'childhood innocence' as if confident that all nursery teachers will respond with four amens. But what is the status of the incantation? A study – *All Things Bright and Beautiful* – written in the seventies? King criticizes Bernstein for the theory of linguistic codes, saying there there is little or no empirical evidence for it, and anyway it doesn't explain anything, even though it pretends that it does (p.89). But all that King says applies to his own claim about the early childhood tradition.

First, the tradition is not a bunch of concepts, still less 'isms'; it is a chronicle of endeavour by people who questioned the received opinion of their day and who cared enough about children to get things done. They were a highly individual bunch of people who thought things out for themselves. The early childhood education tradition is not an ideology which can be summed up in glib phrases. And second, the belief that the study of human development is relevant to teachers of young children, the conviction that even children are individuals, have rights and are entitled to respect, the view that learning can be unforced, pleasurable and still serious, and the principle that young offenders are not to be treated like immoral adults, can all be defended in the open. The early childhood education tradition does not need defending, it needs weeding. It needs attention. The variety and complexity of contributions to the 'common law' tradition over a passage of time have become harder and harder to differentiate, as ideas and practices, once at variance and even opposition, began to merge. There has been inadequate analysis of ideas, which were in any case largely unsupported by evidence from the classroom and constructive reappraisal has not been conspicuous by its presence: the very conditions that could give rise to it – such as a body of evidence to consult – were missing.

Yet, as classroom research gathers momentum and continues to produce evidence that higher quality provision is possible, there is a risk that too much of this tradition might simply be discarded. We believe that the research should be used as a basis for much needed critical analysis – to discover the virtues as well as the vices of that tradition.

The second of the centres is the research field. This is, as we have tried to show, a development of inestimable value. Where early childhood education, like those of the other age-phases, languished for lack of empirical knowledge, now research both large and small scale is burgeoning. We can at last find out what other people are doing, what works and what hasn't yet. For teachers keenly interested in their own profession, inservice courses have changed out of all recognition. We also look forward to a growing body of classroom research in the early years of education which is more thoroughly appropriate to this rich tradition and which captures quality learning experiences, exploring the ways in which these occur in busy classrooms. The forthcoming report and discussion of the Froebel Block Play Project (Gura, 1992) promises to be an – at present rare – example of such research.

The third area is the indispensable one: it comprises the professionals themselves, meeting, comparing notes, reading research and reviving the ideas and lives of people in the movement. Can teachers maintain individual attention? What are the appropriate curricula? What standards are possible? What kinds of behaviour should be tolerated? What successes have there been? What can be done to improve practice? After all, Bennett and Kell (1989) concluded from the evidence of their research that problems of classroom practice, notably ineffective matching, monitoring and diagnosis, result from teachers' 'persistence in attempts to implement and maintain a philosophy of individualization. It is this which is the core of the problem.' (p.85). *Can* something be done?

Positive features

We have tried in this book to look critically at existing research evidence in the context of that tradition of practice and we summarize some of the chief findings here. Variations between schools contain given factors such as age, size and type of building, and ratios between adults and children which influence the quality and nature of the child's learning experience, but it is also clear that the management responses of schools and teachers to these can vary considerably.

In chapters four, five and six structures within the classroom setting were considered and following an evaluation of research concerned with the organization of time, a 'transparent' form of structuring was favoured in which adults in the nursery and reception class take complementary roles to maximise quality interaction with children. Similarly, with respect to spatial considerations a flexible structure was recommended. By grouping materials into areas teachers help to reduce stereotypical play and foster creativity by permitting and encouraging children to combine materials within and between areas.

Research related to the third aspect – task activities – suggests that a common purpose for the use of materials is elusive, and that greater breadth, beyond typical play provision, would enhance the quality of learning. Attention to the activities and conversations of children provided an essential starting point, and an improved partnership with parents was implied in the interests of achieving this. Such classroom structures provide, we suggest, the context for successful tutorial structures, and the weight of research in this field is considered in chapter seven. It strongly indicates the importance of developing structures which allow for genuine negotiation in learning to take place in the classroom. Research evaluation can thus inform critical reflection and provide a basis for the kind of principled practice that keeps things flexible enough to cope with innovation.

The following example illustrates this: a reading of the research conclusions of Tizard and Hughes (1984) or Sylva et al (1980) might, in isolation, indicate that notions such as 'play as learning' and 'free play' should be replaced or diminished in importance. But in our view, this would not be an adequate or appropriate response. These notions should instead be subjected to rigorous discussion, as indeed such research evidence requires, and transformed from the slogans some use them as into topics for proper consideration as classroom strategies. This can only be achieved by:

i) Objective reflection on classroom complexities, assisted by classroom models such as that put forward by Doyle (1986), which together help to take these complexities into account
ii) Reference to a variety of relevant research evidence (considered in chapters five and six) – for example, Tizard and Hughes' own 1984 study, Sylva et al (1980), Hutt et al (1989), Sestini (1987), Davenport (1983) and Dunn and Morgan (1987)
iii) Analysis of the terms 'free', 'play' and 'learning' in this context.

So we take a quite different view from that suggested by our colleague Tina Bruce (1991). She believes that the work of many researchers mentioned here – Bennett, Hutt, Sylva (Oxford Studies) and Tizard and Hughes 'has contributed to a serious undermining of confidence amongst early years professionals.' (p.16). Our view is that if confidence has been undermined it certainly should not have been. We are inclined to agree with the statement made towards the end of the eleventh evaluation report of the Leeds Primary Needs Programme (University of Leeds, 1990):

> Like all (PRINDEPS) reports so far this one's main purpose is formative. It identifies trends, raises issues and draws conclusions of a kind which will support its [the Authority's] commitment to enhancing the quality of primary education in the city's schools but only if those reading and studying the reports are prepared to respond in an open-minded and non-defensive way to what they offer. (p.96).

This corresponds with our earlier comments about the value of class-room research. It surely represents an essential ingredient and aid to teachers in the process of reflection and reappraisal of practice and must contribute to the development and refining of quality.

The value then of such informed discussion as outlined above in the Tizard and Hughes and Sylva examples would come from high-lighting issues which teachers who are seriously concerned to review their work at a structural level ought, in our view, to address. It is, we hope, clear to the reader that we think that concepts fundamental to a learner-centred philosophy are indispensable to good classroom teaching, provided that early years educators are not only receptive to the need for constant re-appraisal and reflection but prepared in the light of research evidence to modify their practice. In the last analysis, education has to be beneficial to children.

The research we have considered has been critical of many aspects of educational provision for young children, notably some kinds of classroom management and the effective promotion of cognitive and language development. From what we think of as a structural perspective we believe that research samples and methods have not taken learner-centred ideas seriously enough and that belief has been reflected in our criticism.

Much of what we have to say is in line with the research of Chris-tine Pascal (1990). Though supportive of early years teachers and acknowledging the restrictions within which they must often work, Pascal found:

> Clear principles, priorities and rationales for practice were generally lacking, which meant that teachers often felt undue

pressure from outside sources. The gap between rhetoric and practice was often enormous (p.30-1).

Though teachers said that play and talk were their curriculum priorities, six out of ten teachers appeared to separate work and play, work, they say, taking place in the mornings, play in the afternoons. In nine out of ten classrooms tables and chairs occupied most space, with all other facilities and equipment arranged around these, giving 'the impression in a majority of cases of a very formal and desk bound environment.' (p.22).

Pascal offered some reasons for this discrepancy between what people said and what they did. These included: lack of status, inadequate support from school and LEA, poor adult/child ratio, miserly resourcing and lack of appropriate training. Such factors are to be taken very seriously of course, and should be addressed. But they are not necessarily impediments to good practice. Where there is a clear rationale for practice, where the teaching team has worked out its priorities, whatever resources are available can be put to better use. Pascal reported:

There were examples of small classrooms with large numbers of children being organized imaginatively and successfully to create an appropriate environment for these young children (p.22).

A further issue is that there are many ways of interpreting research evidence, and the implications drawn by different researchers in respect of similar types of evidence are indicative of the varying values and assumptions which guide their perceptions. The Hutt research and that by Sylva and her colleagues examined principles of free-choice and self-direction and each study found that contrary to the obvious intention, these principles in action, in the settings observed, limited challenge and frequently supported stereotypical play. However, the recommendations they made for improvement, such as overall structure and provision of materials, differed significantly: those of the Hutt study were very much more consistent with a learner-centred approach than Sylva's. While the former made suggestions that would promote the more effective exercise of free-choice and self-direction, the latter made suggestions that would, it seems to us, be more likely to impede such activity.

Aims and values

Finally, we should say what it is we think schools ought to be doing with and for nursery age children. A brief account will go some way towards explaining our view.

First, children have rights. They have rights at home and they have them at school. Having rights means that they are legally protected and are entitled to respect from us and the rest of the people they meet at school. Although it will certainly happen, they are not at school to be changed in temperament or personality and we should beware of trying to do so. Although not owned by parents children are tied emotionally to them and we should respect that bond. Yet we are not just anyone. We are licensed to educate children and from time to time inspected to see that we do it properly. We think our main task is to help children to develop into autonomous people. We hasten to say that we do not consider autonomy a destination, it is a direction, and a rather personal one at that. Each of us travels a different route towards autonomy, which is why helping others develop autonomously means taking them seriously as persons in their own right.

Second, we prefer perspectives to theories; we like loosish structures in which spontaneity and freshness can flourish. Yet respect for children means that one must intervene when it is justified to do so, especially morally. Children are only neutral for a few seconds, if that. Then they become partial. That is what 'natural' means. Partiality means favouring some more than others. It is the way of the world. But schools are different. In school, particularly nursery and first school one learns the difficult lessons of impartiality and what it means to find a place within a community. Schools are also the places where art and music and drama are fostered, where imagination is encouraged. It is the place too for getting things right, or at least, finding out that it matters that things are done well. Above all, perhaps, in the nursery, it is a place for sharing experiences. Though the children will never remember it in later years, it should be the time of their lives.

The responsibilities are all on the side of the teacher. For plainly, though the implication is that she must accept what the child *is*, she is obliged not to accept what the child *says* or *does* when that exceeds certain limits. Conforming to the principle outlined, the teacher is the moral force. It exemplifies the major concern for what might be termed moral autonomy in which the promotion of the individual's rational independence is constrained by the social context within which she operates, and so developed and modified to include not only care and concern for others but interest in and respect for their thoughts and ideas.

In justifying the learner-centred approach in education a concern for the individual has been strongly re-iterated, yet it has been re-defined too. There has been no suggestion that children are in some way protected from teachers, apart from their intrinsic right to be respected. This is a *learner-centred* approach and children are there to be educated. The thrust of the argument is that they should frequently work in collaboration and cooperation (as in the research of Robson, and Hughes and Westgate), and that individuality – a sense of worth, control and unique contribution – is essential for that collaboration to be successful. The teacher charged with encouraging the one must also ensure that she attends to the other.

Therefore a critical thread continuing throughout this book has been a consideration of the role of the adult in the education of young children. It suggests that though the teacher's control is to some extent limited by the 'givens' of the situation – the adult-child ratio being of particular concern – she does in fact have a great deal of influence, sometimes in ways not perceived. An examination of features of structure indicates both how complex classroom organization is and the extent to which this can differ from one classroom to another as a result of the decisions involved. Reflection on structures is crucial to quality education.

The structuring and organization of any classroom are features of the hidden curriculum, but are of special significance in the early years classroom where the distinction between the hidden and the overt curriculum is blurred. Clearly the children are learning from these structures constantly. The more awareness the teacher has, the greater scope there will be for observation of and engagement with her pupils.

Implicit in the forms of structure favoured here and in the conclusive research evidence concerning classroom talk is the importance of the measure of control afforded the child for the achievement of quality learning experiences. Both children and teachers contribute to tutorial structures, that is, the relationships, both intimate and formal, between teachers and individual children. They are the nexuses of learning where ideas are exchanged and challenged.

The school's philosophy, policies and classroom structures can provide the necessary conditions for these tutorial relationships to flourish so that developing the potential of each child can become a firm commitment. It should be kept firmly in mind at the outset when school policies are being developed or reviewed and class teachers reflect on and evaluate their classroom arrangements. Just as plainly, tutorial contexts cannot by-pass these prior considerations, tempting though it may seem, or they will have no foundation on which to operate. Without such a context, it is possible that interaction will be of poor quality and at best haphazard and inconsistent, perhaps something very good but certainly not reliably so. This should not be taken as a criticism of working intuitively with children. On the contrary, intuition is likely to be the very essence of a sensitive approach to tutorial dialogue. However there can be no doubt that it falls far short of providing a rationale for good practice. It is therefore important to appraise interactions which occur within the structure together with a consideration of the overall framework in which this structure is placed. This plays a critical part in establishing such a rationale.

During the course of such appraisals teachers will question their intuitive engagement with the class. What is the basis for their interaction with children? To seek answers to this they will want to consider their assumptions, developed during the period of training and subsequently working with children. It will also be necessary to reflect on expectations accumulated as a result of previous experiences as well as those arising from present classroom experience. This kind of analysis will be supportive of the exercise of intuition as skilled expertise on the part of the teacher. We think that spontaneity with children is essential, and is sacrificed at great expense in terms of the process of worthwhile learning. Entering into young children's thinking and their stories is the key to the sensitive opening up of their worlds.

In conclusion, we believe we can find no apter way of expressing the idea that is at the heart of this book than by quoting a remark from Vivian Paley again. This time it is from *The Boy Who Would Be A Helicopter* (1990):

We have not heard such ordinary talk before from Jason, yet at home he probably converses in this manner all the time. We judge and evaluate Jason in a place where he has not been comfortable enough to engage in good conversations. In school he has felt in need of repairs. I must always assume, with any child, that school is the source of whatever problems exist in school before looking elsewhere.

Bibliography

Alexander, R. (1988). 'Garden or Jungle? Teacher Development and Informal Primary Education'. In Blyth A., *Informal Primary Education Today*, Lewes: Falmer Press.

Alexander, R. (1991). *Primary Education in Leeds: Briefing and Summary*, Leeds: Leeds University Press.

Athey, C. (1981). 'Parental Involvement in Nursery Education'. *Early Child Development and Care*, 7(4): 353-367.

Atkins, J. (1981). 'Is Play Quite the Thing?' *Times Educational Supplement*, 9.9.81.

Bailey, C. (1975). 'Knowledge of Others and Concern for Others'. In Elliott, J. and Pring, R. (eds) *Social Education and Social Understanding*, London: University of London Press.

Beardsley, G. (1989). 'Play: New Ways of Looking'. In *Early Years: Journal of TACTYC*, 9(2): 17-20.

Bennett, C. (1985). 'Paint Pots or Promotion: Art Teachers' Attitudes Towards School'. In Ball, S.J. and Goodson, I. *Teachers' Lives and Careers*, Lewes: Falmer Press.

Bennett, N., Desforges, C., Cockburn, A. and Wilkinson, B. (1984). *The Quality of Pupil Learning Experiences*, London: Lawrence Erlbaum Associates.

Bennett, N., Desforges, C., Cockburn, A. and Wilkinson, B. (1988). 'The Experienced Curriculum'. In Clarkson, M. *Emerging Issues in Primary Education*, Lewes: Falmer Press.

Bennett, N. and Kell, J. (1989). *A Good Start? Four Year Olds in Infant Schools*, Oxford: Blackwell.

Bilton, H. *The Development and Significance of the Nursery Garden and Outdoor Play Area*, Unpublished MA dissertation, Roehampton Institute, University Of Surrey.

Blenkin, G. and Kelly, A.V. (eds.) (1987). *The Primary Curriculum in Action*, London: Paul Chapman.

Blenkin, G. & Kelly, A.V. (eds) (1987). *Early Childhood Education*, London: Paul Chapman.

Blenkin, G. (1988). 'Education and Development: Some Implications for the Curriculum in the Early Years'. In Blyth, A. (ed.) *Informal Primary Education Today*, Lewes: Falmer Press.

Blyth, A. (ed.) (1988). *Informal Education Today*, Lewes: Falmer Press.

Brett, M. (1991). *Early Childhood Education: A Practitioner's Attempt to Untangle the Theoretical Roots of her Practice*, Unpublished MA Dissertation, Roehampton Institute, University of Surrey.

Board of Education, (1933). *Report of the Consultative Committee on Infant and Nursery Schools*, London: HMSO.

Booth, T., Swann, W., Masterton, M. and Potts, P. (eds.) (1992). *Policies For Diversity in Education*, London and New York: Routledge.

Bower, T. (1981). 'Language Development in Infancy'. In Roberts, M. and Tamburrini, J. (eds.) *Child Development 0-5*, Edinburgh: Holmes McDougall.

Brearley, M. (ed.) (1969). *Fundamentals in the First School*. Oxford: Blackwell.

Brice-Heath, S. (1982). 'Questioning at Home and at School: a Comparative Study'. In Hammersley, M. (ed.) *1986 Case Studies in Classroom Research*, Milton Keynes and Philadelphia, Open University Press.

Brown, S. and Wake, R. (eds.) (1988). *Education in Transition: What Role For Research?*, Edinburgh: Scottish Council For Research in Education.

Brubacher, J. (1962). *Modern Philosophies of Education*, 3rd Edition, New York and London: McGraw-Hill.

Bruce, T. (1987). *Early Childhood Education*, Sevenoaks, Kent: Hodder & Stoughton.

Bruce, T. (1991). *Time To Play in Early Childhood Education*, London: Hodder & Stoughton.

Bruner, J. (1983). *Child's Talk: Learning to Use Language*, Oxford: Oxford University Press.

Bruner, J. and Haste, H. (1987). *Making Sense*, London and New York: Methuen.

Bullough, R.V., Knowles, J. and Crow, N. (1991). *Emerging as a Teacher*, London and New York: Routledge.

Campbell, J. (1988). 'The "Collegial" Primary School'. In M. Clarkson (ed.) *Emerging Issues in Primary Education*, Lewes: Falmer Press.

Cashdan, A. and Meadows, S. (1983). *Teaching Styles in Nursery Education: Final Report of Grant No. AR 3456*, London: SSRC.

Clark, M. (1983). 'Early Education: Issues and Evidence'. *Educational Review*, 35(2): 113-119.

Clark, M., (1988). *Children Under Five: Educational Research and Evidence*, London: Gordon & Breach Science Publishers.

Clarkson, M. (ed.) (1988). *Emerging Issues in Primary Education*, Lewes: Falmer Press.

Cohen, A. and Cohen L. (eds.) (1986). *Primary Education: A Sourcebook for Teachers*, London: Harper Education.

Cohen, A. and Cohen, L. (eds.) (1988). *Early Education: The Pre-School Years. A Sourcebook for Teachers*, London: Paul Chapman.

Coulson, A. (1990). 'Primary School Headship: A Review of Research'. In Saran, R. and Trafford, V. (eds.) *Research in Education Management and Policy*, Falmer Press. .

Curtis, A. (1986). *Curriculum for the Pre-School Child*, Windsor: NFER-Nelson.

Davenport, E. (1983). 'The Play of Sikh Children in a Nursery Class and at Home'. *Educational Review*, 35(2): 127-139.

Desforges, C., (ed.) (1989). *Early Childhood Education*, Edinburgh: Scottish Academic Press.

Dimitracopoulou, I. (1990). *Conversational Competence and Social Development*, Cambridge: Cambridge University Press.

Dolley, D. and Wheldall, K., (1987). '"Talking to Teacher" – Using Incidental Teaching to Encourage Child Initiations in the Nursery classroom: a case study'. *Child Language Teaching and Therapy*, 3(3): 277-292.

Donaldson, M. (1978). *Children's Minds*, London: Fontana.

Dowling, M. (1988). *Education 3-5: A Teachers' Handbook*, London: Paul Chapman.

Doyle, W. (1979). 'Classroom Tasks and Student Abilities'. In Peterson, P. and Walberg, H. J. (eds.), *Research on Teaching: Concepts, Findings and Implications*, Berkeley, Calif: McCutchan.

Doyle, W. (1979). 'Classroom Effects'. *Theory Into Practice*, Vol XVIII (3).

Doyle, W. (1983). 'Academic Work'. *Review of Educational Research*, 53(2): 159-99.

Doyle, W. (1984). 'How Order is achieved in classrooms'. *Journal of Curriculum Studies*, 16(3).

Doyle, W. (1986a). 'Classroom Organisation and Management'. In Wittrock, M. (ed.) *3rd Handbook of Research on Teaching*, New York: Macmillan.

Doyle, W. (1986b). 'Content Representation in Teachers' Definitions of Academic Work'. *Journal of Curriculum Studies*, 18(4).

Doyle, W. (1986c) 'Academic Tasks in Classrooms'. In Hammersley, M. (ed.) *Case Studies in Classroom Research*, Milton Keynes and Philadelphia: Open University Press.

Duckworth, E. (1979) 'Either We're too Early and They Can't Learn it or We're too Late and They Know it Already: The Dilemma of Applying Piaget'. In *Harvard Education Review* 49 (3): 297 – 312.

Dunn, S. and Morgan, V. (1987). 'Nursery and Infant School Play Patterns: Sex-Related Differences'. *British Educational Research Journal*, 13(3): 271 – 281. .

Dye, J. (1984). 'Early Education Matters: a Study of Pre-School Curriculum Content'. In *Educational Research*, 26(2): 95-105.

Early Years Curriculum Group, (1989). *The Early Years Curriculum and the National Curriculum*, Stoke on Trent: Trentham Books.

Edwards, D. and Mercer, N. (1987). *Common Knowledge: The Development of Understanding in the Classroom*, London and New York: Methuen.

Eyken, W. Van Der, (1982). *The Education of Three- to Eight-Year-Olds in the Eighties*, Windsor, NFER.

Eyken, W. Van Der, (1984). 'Pre-Schooling in Britain: A National Study of Institutional Provision for under-fives in England, Scotland and Wales'. In *Early Child Development and Care*.

Galton, M., Simon, B. and Croll, P., (1980). *Inside the Primary Classroom*, London: Routledge & Kegan Paul.

Galton, M. and Simon, B., (eds.) (1980). *Progress and Performance in the Primary Classroom*, London: Routledge & Kegan Paul.

Galton, M. and Willcocks, J. (eds.) (1983). *Moving From the Primary Classroom*, London: Routledge & Kegan Paul.

126

Galton, M. (1989). *Teaching in the Primary School*, London: David Fulton.

Gammage, P. (1986). 'Gone but not Forgotten: Aspirations of English Early Childhood Education', in 'Education and the Four-Year-Old: A Cause for Concern'. In *TACTYC Special Issue*, Manchester.

Gammage, P. (1988). 'Primary School Practice Beyond Plowden'. In Blyth, A., *Informal Primary Education Today*, Lewes: Falmer Press.

Gardner, D. (1969). *Susan Isaacs: The First Biography*, London: Methuen.

Gibson, R. (1984). *Structuralism and Education*, London: Hodder and Stoughton.

Golby, M. (1988) 'Traditions in Primary Education'. In Clarkson, M., (ed.) *Emerging Issues in Primary Education*, Lewes: Falmer Press.

Gura, P. (ed.) (1992). *Exploring Learning: Young Children and Block Play*, London: Paul Chapman.

Hammersley, M. (ed.) (1986). *Case Studies in Classroom Research*, Milton Keynes and Philadelphia: Open University Press.

Hartley, D. (1987). 'The Time of Their Lives: Bureaucracy and the Nursery School'. In Pollard, A. (ed.) *Children and their Primary Schools*, Lewes: Falmer Press.

Hawkes, T. (1977). *Structuralism and Semiotics*, London: Methuen.

Hill, T, (1989). *Managing Primary Schools*, London: David Fulton.

HMI (1989). *Aspects of Primary Education. The Education of Children Under Five*, London: HMSO.

House of Commons (1988). *First Report of the Education, Science and Arts Committee on Educational Provision for the Under Fives*, London: HMSO.

Hughes, M. and Grieve, R. (1988). 'On Asking Children Bizarre Questions'. In Cohen, A. and Cohen, L. (eds.) *Early Education: The Pre-school Years*, London: Paul Chapman.

Hughes, M. and Westgate, D. (1988). 'Re-appraising Talk in Nursery and Reception Classes'. *Education 3-13*, 16(2): 9-15.

Hutt, C. (1966) 'Exploration and Play in Children'. *Play Exploration and Territory in Mammals*, Symposium of the Zoological Society of London, 18.

Hutt, C. (1979). *Play in the Under Fives: Form, Development and Function*, New York: Brunner/Mazel.

Hutt, C. (1981). 'Towards a Taxonomy and Conceptual Model of Play'. In Day, H. I., (ed.) *Advances in Intrinsic Motivation and Aesthetics*. New York: Plenum Press.

Hutt, S., Tyler, S., Hutt, C. and Christopherson, H., (1989). *Play, Exploration and Learning: a Natural History of the Pre-School*, London and New York: Routledge.

Jackson, M. (1987) 'Making Sense of School'. In Pollard, A. *Children and their Primary Schools*, Lewes: Falmer Press.

Katz, L. (1988). *Dilemmas in Early Childhood Work*, References are to a Lecture at Froebel Institute College, May 17, 1988.

King, R. (1982). 'Multiple Realities and their Reproduction in Infants' Classrooms'. In Richards, C. (ed.) *New Directions in Primary Education*, Lewes: Falmer Press.

King, R. (1988). 'Informality, Ideology and Infants' Schooling'. In Blyth, A., *Informal Primary Education Today*, Lewes: Falmer Press.

Liebschner, J. (1992). *Foundations of Progressive Education: The History of the National Froebel Society*, Cambridge: Lutterworth Press.

McCreery, E. (1991). *An Investigation into the Effects of the 1988 Education Reform Act on Collective Worship in Primary Schools*, Unpublished MA Dissertation, Roehampton Institute, University of Surrey.

Manning, M. and Herrmann, J. (1988). 'The Relationship of Problem Children in Nursery Schools'. In Cohen, A. and Cohen, L. (eds.) *Early Education: The Pre-School Years*, London: Paul Chapman.

Meadows, S. and Cashdan, A.(1982) 'Children's Free Play in Nursery Schools', Unpublished Paper presented to the *British Psychological Society: Developmental Section*.

Meadows, S. and Cashdan, A. (1988) *Helping Children Learn: Contributions to a Cognitive Curriculum*, London: David Fulton.

Nash, B. (1981) 'The Effects of Classroom Spatial Organization on Four- and Five-Year-Old Children's Learning'. In *British Journal of Educational Psychology*, 51: 144-155.

NCC, (1989) 'A Framework for the Primary Curriculum'. In *Curriculum Guidance*, York: NCC.

Nias, J., Southworth, G., and Yeomans, R. (1989). *Staff Relationships in the Primary School*, London: Cassell.

Nias, J. (1989). *Primary Teachers Talking: A Study of Teaching As Work*, London: Routledge.

Northam, J. (1988). 'The 'Myth' of the Pre-School'. In Cohen, A. and Cohen L. (eds.) *Early Education: The Pre-School Years*, London: Paul Chapman.

Osborn, A. and Millbank, J. (1987) *The Effects of Early Education*, Oxford: The Clarendon Press.

Paley, V. (1981). *Wally's Stories*, Cambridge, Mass. and London: Harvard University Press .

Paley, V.(1986). 'On Listening To What Children Say'. *In Harvard Educational Review*, 56(2): 122-131.

Paley, V. (1990). *The Boy Who Would Be A Helicopter*, Cambridge, Mass. and London: Harvard University Press.

Pascal, C. (1989). 'What's All This Fuss About The Early Years?' In *Early Years: Journal of TACTYC*, 9 (2): 5-10.

Pascal, C.(1990). *Under-Fives in the Infant Classroom*, Stoke-on-Trent: Trentham Books.

Passmore, J. (1984). 'Academic Ethics?'. *Journal of Applied Philosophy*, 1(1).

Peters, R. (1966). *Ethics and Education*, George Allen & Unwin.

Peters, R. (1974). *Psychology and Ethical Development*, London: Unwin University Books.

Piaget, J. (1971). *Structuralism*, tr. Maschler, C. London: RKP.

Pound, L. (1986). *Perceptions of Nursery Practice: An Exploration of Nursery Teacher's Views of the Curriculum*, Unpublished MA dissertation, Roehampton Institute and University of Surrey.

Robson, B. (1983). 'Encouraging Dialogue in Pre-School Units: The Role of the Pink Pamfer'. In *Educational Review*, Vol 35, No 2, pp 141-147.

Robson, S. (1990). *Developing Autonomous Children in the First School*, Unpublished MA Dissertation, Roehampton Institute and University of Surrey.

Scholes, R., (1974). *Structuralism in Literature*, New Haven and London: Yale University Press.

Schon, D. (1983). *The Reflective Practitioner: How Professionals Think in Action*, New York: Basic Books.

Schon, D. (1987). *Educating the Reflective Practitioner: Toward a New Design for Teaching and Learning in the Professions*, San Francisco, CA: Jossey-Bass.

Schostak, J. (1987). 'As You Mean to go on: First Days at School'. In Booth, T. and Coulby, D. (eds.) *Producing and Reducing Disaffection*, Milton Keynes: Open University Press.

Sestini, E. (1987). 'The Quality of the Learning Experiences of Four-Year-Olds in Nursery and Infant Classes'. In *Four-Year-Olds in School: Policy and Practice*, Slough: NFER/SCDC.

Shipman, M. (1985). *The Management of Learning in the Classroom*, Sevenoaks, Kent: Hodder & Stoughton.

Snow, C. (1979). 'The Development of Conversation Between Mothers and Babies'. In Lee, V. *Language Development*, London and Milton Keynes: Croom Helm.

Southworth, G. (1987). *Readings in Primary School Management*, Lewes: Falmer Press.

Stevenson, C. (1987). 'The Young Four-Year-Old in Nursery and Infant Classes: Challenges and Constraints'. In *Four Year Olds in School: Policy and Practice*, NFER/SCDC.

Sylva, K., Roy, C. and Painter, M. (1980). *Childwatching at Playgroup and Nursery School*, London, Grant McIntyre.

Sylva, K. (1986). 'Structure in the Classroom'. In *TACTYC: 'National Conference at Manchester Special Issue: The Education of Four-Year-Olds: A Cause for Concern'*.

Tamburrini, J. (1981). 'Teaching Style in Relation to Play in the Nursery School'. In Roberts, M. and Tamburrini, J. (eds.) *Child Development 0-5*, Edinburgh, Holmes McDougal.

Tamburrini, J. (1982). 'New Directions in Nursery School Education'. In Richards, C. (ed) *New Directions in Primary Education*, Lewes: Falmer Press, also in Cohen, A and Cohen, L (eds.) *Early Education: The Pre-School Years*, London, Paul Chapman.

Tattum, D. and Tattum, E. (1990). *Social Education and Personal Development in the Primary School*, London: David Fulton.

Tizard, B. and Hughes M. (1984). *Young Children Learning*, London: Fontana.

University of Leeds Primary Needs Independent Evaluation Project (1990). *Teachers and Children in PNP Classroom Evaluation. Report Eleven*, Leeds: Leeds University Press.

Walford, G. (ed.) (1991). *Doing Educational Research*, London and New York, Routledge.

Wallace, M. (1988). 'Towards a Collegiate Approach to Curriculum Management in Primary and Middle School'. *School Organisation*, 8(1).

Webb, L. (1974). *Purpose and Practice in Nursery Education*, Oxford: Blackwell.

Weikart, D., Epstein, A., Schweinhart, L. and Bond J. (1978). *The Ypsilanti Perry Pre-School Project: Pre-School Years and Longitudinal Results Through Fourth Grade*, Monograph 3, Michigan: High/Scope Press.

Weikhart, D. (1988). 'A Perspective in High/Scope's Early Education Research'. In *Early Child Development and Care* 33: 29-40.

Wells, G. and Wells, J. (1984). 'Talking and Learning' In *English in Education*, 18(1): 28-38.

Wells, G. (1986). *The Meaning Makers*, London: Hodder & Stoughton.

Williams, M. (1986). *Teachers' Responses to Children's Initiatives in Verbal Interactions*, Unpublished MA dissertation, Roehampton Institute and University of Surrey.

Willig, J. (1990). *Children's Concepts and the Primary Curriculum* London: Paul Chapman.

Wood, D. et al (1980). *Working With Under Fives*, London: McIntyre.

Wood, H. and Wood, D. (1987). 'Questioning the Pre-School Child'. In Cohen, A. and Cohen, L. (eds) *Early Education: The Pre-School Years*, London: Paul Chapman.

Woodhead, M. (1987). 'The Needs of Children: Is There Any Value in the Concept?'. In *Oxford Review of Education*, 13(2).

Woodhead, M. and Weikart, D., (1987). 'Comparative Studies in Pre-School Education'. In *Encyclopaedia of Comparative Education*, Oxford: Pergamon Press.

Zigler, E., (1987). 'Formal Schooling for Four-Year-Olds? No.' In *American Psychologist*, 42: 254-260.

Name Index

Main Topics